So...

From

Heaven

by

TIMOTHY J. E. CROSS
BA, BD, Th.D, PGCE

AMBASSADOR

Scent from Heaven
© Copyright 1994 Timothy J. E. Cross

ISBN 0-907927-88-2

Published by

Ambassador Productions Limited
Providence House
16 Hillview Avenue
Belfast BT5 6JR

Contents

Dedicated to
Jeremy ~ brother and best friend

Author's Preface

The following pages consist of a devotional, typological and factual study of the ever blessed Person of Christ, along with some of the blessings He imparts to all who trust in His redeeming blood. It was a great blessing for me to prepare, and my prayer is that it will prove to be the same to a wider readership. May the Lord be pleased to take up this labour of love *to grant to those who mourn in Zion - to give them a garland instead of ashes, the oil of gladness instead of mourning, the mantle of praise instead of a faint spirit* (Isaiah 61:3).

A big "thank you" to Mr. Ernest Brown, Belfast, for taking time from a very busy schedule to read through the proofs.

Timothy J. E. Cross
Cardiff, Wales.

CHAPTER ONE

The Fragrance Of The Sacred Perfume

THE ANOINTING OIL : THE CHRISM

Exodus 30:22-38 details for us both the constitution and use of a certain *sacred anointing oil blended as by the perfumer; a holy oil it shall be* (25). This special and fragrant ointment owes its constitution and manufacture to none other than the Lord Himself (22), Who instructed Moses with the sacred recipe for this unique oil. All this was over three thousand years ago now. The people of Israel were in the wilderness, having been delivered miraculously from slavery in Egypt by the blood of a lamb - that clear type of the Lord Jesus Christ. The fragrant oil in question was absolutely unique. There was *no other like it in composition, it is holy and shall be holy to you* (32). Here then, amazing as it sounds, we are dealing with the Divine perfume of heaven.

THE AROMATIC OINTMENT : THE CONSTITUTION

The anointing oil was a compound of five of the *finest spices: of liquid myrrh ... sweet smelling cinnamon ... aro-*

matic cane ... *cassia* ... *and of olive oil*, all blended into one luxurious substance. The number five in the Bible speaks to us of Divine grace - God's unmerited goodwill towards the undeserving and ill deserving such as we are. Four speaks to us of the world - *the four corners of the earth* (Revelation 7:1), and one is the number of God Himself - *Hear O Israel: The Lord our God, the Lord is One* (Mark 12:29). 1 + 4 = 5, thus five speaks of God acting on the world in Divine grace (c.f. the five Levitical offerings of Leviticus 1-7; the five loaves with which Jesus fed the multitudes in John 6:1-14 and the *five smooth stones* (1 Samuel 16:40) at the time when David slew Goliath.) When we think of Divine grace, our minds immediately turn to *the God of all grace* (1 Peter 5:10) Who revealed Himself to Moses at this time as *The Lord, the Lord, a God merciful and gracious, slow to anger, and abounding in steadfast love and faithfulness* (Exodus 34:6). But how much more light do we have than Moses! We are living in the days after God became Man in the Person of His Son, the Lord Jesus Christ. *From His fullness have we all received grace upon grace. For the law was given through Moses; grace and truth came through Jesus Christ. No one has ever seen God; (man shall not see Me and live* [Exodus 33:20]) *the only Son Who is in the bosom of the Father, He has made Him known* (John 1:16-18).

THE ANOINTED ONE : THE CHRIST

The fragrant anointing oil however seems to speak beyond itself and give us many illustrations and insights into the Christ Himself. The chrism speaks of Christ - the anointing oil tells of the Anointed One, He Who said of Himself that *Moses ... wrote of Me* (John 5:46), as well as referring to Himself as *Him Whom the Father consecrated and sent into the world* (John 10:36).

Those who know Christ in all His fragrant loveliness, along with all the saving benefits which He bestows, find some articulation in using the words of the ancient love poem - a poem which Christians have historically considered as speaking of our heavenly Bride-groom:- *Your anointing oils are fragrant, your Name is oil poured out* (Song of Solomon 1:3). Jesus truly is the long anticipated Christ, and the title 'Christ' literally means 'Christos/the Anointed One.'

In a turning point in the Gospel accounts, Peter was led to confess to Jesus *"You are the Christ, the Son of the living God"* (Matthew 16:16). *Your Name is oil poured out* reminds us again of Him, and His *blood of the New Covenant which is poured out for many for the forgiveness of sins* (Matthew 26:28). His Name truly is the Name which is above every name and one day at the *Name of Jesus every knee should bow, in heaven and on earth and under the earth and every tongue confess that Jesus Christ is Lord to the glory of God the Father* (Philippians 2:10,11).

Let us then look at this most holy Anointed One in the sacred offices for which He was anointed to act as the only Redeemer of God's elect:-

THE ANTICIPATED OFFICE : THE CONSECRATION

In Old Testament times, prophets, priests and kings were all anointed with oil at the beginning of their ministries. This anointing was symbolic of their being anointed with the Holy Spirit, Who thus set them apart and consecrated them for their office and role, equipping them for their specific tasks. Thus in the passage with which we began we read God's command to Moses that with the sacred oil *You shall anoint Aaron and his sons, and consecrate them, that they may serve Me as priests* (Exodus 30:30).

9

In 1 Samuel 16:13 we read of Israel's greatest king to be:-
Then Samuel took the horn of oil, and anointed him (David)
*... and the Spirit of the Lord came mightily upon David from
that day forward.*

As regards the office of prophet, note 1 Kings 19:16.
Elijah the prophet was there told *Elishah the son of Shaphat
... you shall anoint to be prophet in your place.*

THE ARRIVED ONE : THE COMING

Jesus is the long anticipated Christ, the Anointed One; and
He fulfils the offices of prophet, priest and king supremely, in
His one Divine Person.

Jesus is the Anointed One. Peter preached *how God
anointed Jesus of Nazareth with the Holy Spirit and with
power* (Acts 10:38). Jesus Himself claimed to fulfil the
prophecy of Isaiah when he wrote *The Spirit of the Lord is
upon Me, because He has anointed Me to preach good news
to the poor* (Luke 4:18), and we recall the inauguration of
Jesus's ministry at His baptism in the Jordan when *the Holy
Spirit descended upon Him in bodily form, as a dove* (Luke
3:22).

THE ANOINTED ONE : THE CHRIST

The anointing oil was thus a very special oil, used only for
the anointing to the special tasks of prophet, priest and king.
Jesus fulfils all three of these offices. He is the especially
Anointed One - anointed to be the only Redeemer of God's
elect. No wonder the Psalmist wrote of Him:- *God has
anointed You with the oil of gladness above Your fellows;
Your robes are all fragrant with myrrh and aloes and cassia*
(Psalm 45:7,8). He is our Prophet, Priest and King. How? Let
the Shorter Catechism answer:-

THE ANNOTED ONE : THE CATECHISM

"Christ executeth the office of a prophet in revealing to us by His Word and Spirit the will of God for our salvation.

"Christ executeth the office of a priest in His once offering up of Himself a sacrifice to satisfy divine justice, and reconcile us to God; and in making continual intercession for us.

"Christ executeth the office of a king in subduing us to Himself, in ruling and defending us, and in restraining and conquering all His and our enemies."

THE ACCLAIMED ONE : THE CANTICLE

The anointing chrism was absolutely unique in its constitution and purpose. How much more, however, is this so with God's Anointed Christ. He too is unique in His character and purpose. He only is the Saviour of sinners, and Christ as our Redeemer, executes the offices of a prophet, priest and king, both in His estate of humiliation and exaltation.

The anointing oil : the Anointed One. How sweet the Name of Jesus sounds in a believer's ear. *Your anointing oils are fragrant, Your Name is oil poured out* (Song of Solomon 1:3).

> *His fragrant being, all replete*
> *with myrrh and aloes and cassia sweet*
> *all blending in God's lovely Son*
> *This is our beloved One.*

CHAPTER TWO

The Fragrance Of The Sacrificing Priests

And you shall anoint Aaron and his sons, and consecrate
them, that they may serve Me as priests
(Exodus 30:30).

THE INSTITUTION OF THE PRIESTLY SYSTEM

The verse above informs us that the fragrant anointing oil
was functional as well as beautiful. There was more to it than
just an agreeable odour. It was for the express purpose of
anointing Aaron and his sons to consecrate them to serve in
the capacity of priests. The priesthood of Aaron and his sons
was integral to the whole Old Testament economy - and
likewise the priesthood of Christ, our Great High Priest, is
integral to the whole New Testament economy in the present
age of grace. Christ is the consummation and fulfilment of all
that the Old Testament priesthood foreshadowed and por-
trayed.

At His baptism in the river Jordan, Jesus was especially
endowed and anointed with the Holy Spirit as He began His
priestly ministry which was to culminate in His once and for

all offering up of Himself as an atoning sacrifice on Calvary's cross. There, in Jordan's waters *the Holy Spirit descended upon Him in bodily form, as a dove* (Luke 3:22) and Christ's priestly ministry began. The priesthood of Christ is a blessed meditation, bringing to the soul much assurance and godly comfort, as it tells us of the Saving Work which He accomplished on our behalf - as well as the Work which He continues to do in heaven for us now at God's right hand. Christ's priesthood is *the source of eternal salvation to all who obey Him* (Hebrews 5:9), so let us now take heed to the injunction to *consider Jesus, the apostle and high priest of our confession* (Hebrews 3:1).

THE DEFINITION OF THE PRIESTLY SERVICE

Every high priest chosen from among men is appointed to act on behalf of men in relation to God, to offer gifts and sacrifices for sins (Hebrews 5:1). A concise definition of Christ's priestly service is given in Q.25 of the Shorter Catechism. It asks "How doth Christ execute the office of a priest?" and answers "Christ executeth the office of a priest in His once offering up of Himself a sacrifice to satisfy divine justice, and reconcile us to God, and in making continued intercession for us." From this we see that Christ's priesthood is both past and present, completed and continuous. His death on the Cross in the past was a completed sacrifice, never to be repeated - but His intercession for us now is continuous, and indeed will continue until the dawning of the new age, when all the elect will be saved to sin no more, having no need of Christ's continuing intercession.

THE EXPIATION OF THE PRIESTLY SACRIFICE

Blood sacrifice was central to the Old Testament priesthood. A key verse of the Old Testament - if not the whole

Bible - is Leviticus 17:11:- *For the life of the flesh is in the blood; and I have given it for you upon the altar to make atonement for your souls; for it is the blood that makes atonement, by reason of the life.* The whole sacrificial system gave God's Old Testament people object lessons in the absolute severity of sin. A holy God just has to punish sin - or pardon it justly if the sinner is to live. The Bible teaches clearly *the wages of sin is death* (Romans 6:23), and blood sacrifice shows that this is indeed so. Blood sacrifice also, however, gave the people of Israel object lessons in the sheer mercy of God. The sacrifices were of God's mercy. In them, God provided a substitute for the sinner. Instead of the sinner dying for his own sins, God's mercy allowed that an innocent animal could die in the place of the sinner, his blood thus covering/making atonement for his sin. This may seem a very drastic way to deal with sin - but sin in God's eyes is very drastic. In summary, at this time in history, innocent, unblemished animals were taken to the priests who then slew them on the altar of sacrifice to take away the guilt of the sinner. The sacrifices taught the Divine way of expiation.

The problem for the thinking Old Testament saint however, may be stated thus. "Can I be sure that my sins are forgiven and that I have peace with God?" The sacrificial system itself, although bringing the guilty conscience a measure of relief, gave none of the desired assurance. It went on year after year as a reminder of its imperfection:- *it can never, by the same sacrifices which are continually offered year after year, make perfect those who draw near. Otherwise would they not have ceased to be offered? If the worshippers had once been cleansed, they would no longer have any consciousness of sin. But in these sacrifices there is a reminder of sin year after year. For it is impossible that the blood of bulls and goats should take away sins* (Hebrews 10:1-3). The Old Testament sacrifices were temporary. They pointed forward to and anticipated the One sacrifice which Christ our great high priest, offered on the altar of Calvary. This is the Sacrifice which ends all sacrifices and atones for sins forever!

> *Not all the blood of beasts*
> *On Jewish altars slain*
> *Could give the guilty conscience peace*
> *Or wash away the stain*
>
> *But Christ the heavenly Lamb*
> *Takes all our guilt away*
> *A sacrifice of nobler name*
> *And richer blood than they.*

THE PERFECTION OF THE PRIESTLY SUBSTANCE

Yes, Christ's death on the cross brought an end to the Old Testament priesthood and its sacrificial system. Interestingly, God allowed the historic temple in Jerusalem to be destroyed by the Romans in 70 AD. It has never since been rebuilt - and it never need be rebuilt, as Christ, our great high priest has offered Himself as a perfect sacrifice on Calvary's altar. Additional sacrifices are thus blasphemous, undermining the perfection of Christ's Work. *He has appeared once for all at the end of the age to put away sin by the sacrifice of Himself.* (Hebrews 9:26).

Here then, we mix our metaphors. The Priest is also the Victim. The Offerer is also *the Lamb of God Who takes away the sin of the world* (John 1:29). Hebrews 10:11,12 summarises for us, by way of contrast, the total perfection of Christ's sacrifice at Calvary:- *every priest stands daily at his service offering repeatedly the same sacrifices which can never take away sins. But when Christ had offered for all time a single sacrifice for sins, He sat down at the right hand of God.*

THE DURATION OF THE PRIEST'S SUPREMACY

Christ's sacrifice on the cross was a perfect Work. He Himself said of it *"It is finished"* (John 19:30, 'Tetelestai' in the Greek). This finished Work of Christ, as we have already intimated, brought an end to the Old Testament sacrificial system. It was all rendered unnecessary by Christ. His finished Work was perfect - and you cannot add to perfection. In His so called 'High Priestly prayer' He stated *I glorified Thee on earth, having accomplished the work which Thou gavest Me to do* (John 17:4).

> *No blood, no altar now*
> *The sacrifice is o'er*
> *No flame, no smoke ascends on high*
> *The lamb is slain no more*
> *For richer blood has flowed from nobler veins*
> *To purge the soul from guilt and cleanse the*
> *reddest stains.*

THE INTERCESSION OF THE PRIESTLY SAVIOUR

It is not blasphemous if we say that there is an unfinished aspect to Christ's priestly Work. There is an activity which He continues to do to make our salvation sure - namely His work of intercession for His Own:- *He holds His priesthood permanently, because He continues for ever. Consequently He is able for all time to save those who draw near to God through Him since He always lives to make intercession for them* (Hebrews 7:24,25).

Christ's intercession thus continues. The Old Testament prophesied of Him *The Lord has sworn and will not change His mind, "You are a priest for ever after the order of Melchizedek"* (Psalm 110:4). Mysterious Melchizedek, a priest/king, comes on and off the stage very briefly, way back in Genesis 14. *He is first, by translation of his name, king of righteousness, and then he is also king of Salem, that is, king of peace* (Hebrews 7:2). 'Tsedek is' the Hebrew for righteousness. Christ is our righteousness! We have no righteousness of our own to fit us for God's presence - *The Lord is our righteousness* (Jeremiah 23:6). Melchizedek was also King of Salem. Salem (Jerusalem) is derived from 'Shalom' or 'peace.' It is written of Jesus that *He is our peace* (Ephesians 2:14). In the Bible, righteousness and peace are often linked as cause and effect - a*nd the effect of righteousness will be peace, and the result of righteousness quietness and trust for ever* (Isaiah 32:17). Both of these are brought out in Romans 5:1. Christ's death and resurrection reckons us righteous in God's sight, i.e. it 'justifies' us. *Therefore since we are justified by faith we have peace with God through our Lord Jesus Christ.*

Christ also resembles Melchizedek in that it is written of Melchizedek *He is without father or mother or genealogy, and has neither beginning of days nor end of life, but resembling the Son of God he continues a priest for ever* (Hebrews 7:3). The same Jesus Who died for our sins now sits at God's right hand and intercedes for His Own. He thus not only saves, but He keeps - He keeps us in the good of the Calvary blessings. Says Louis Berkhof :-

"There is ... a connection between the sacrificial work at the brazen altar and the symbolical intercession at the golden altar. The fact that the incense might be burned only on living coals taken from the altar of burnt offering was an indication of the fact that the intercession was based on the sacrifice and would be effective in no other way. This clearly indicates that the intercessory work of Christ in heaven is based on His accomplished sacrificial work, and is acceptable only on that basis." (SYSTEMATIC THEOLOGY, Banner of Truth, 1958, p.400). We marvel anew at the unity between the two testaments.

The work of Calvary was perfect and complete. But we are anything but perfect, and would soon fall away if it were not for the continual intercession of Christ at God's right hand. *If while we were enemies we were reconciled to God by the death of His Son, much more, now that we are reconciled, shall we be saved by His life* (Romans 5:10). *It is Christ Jesus Who died, yes, Who was raised from the dead, Who is at the right hand of God, Who indeed intercedes for us* (Romans 8:34); *we have an advocate with the Father ... and He is the propitiation for our sins* (1 John 2:1,2).

What a comfort it is to have a priest such as this! He is praying for us right now - and His prayers are always heard. Weak and prone to fall as we are, we have a great need for His priestly intercession; but in Christ we have a great High Priest interceding to meet our need. Praise His name! He will continue this unending, unfinished work until we are not just eternally saved but eternally safe! - safe at last in His glorious presence, free from not only the penalty and power, but also from the very presence of sin.

THE BENEDICTION OF THE PRIEST'S SAINTS

Jesus is our great high priest, and we have only paddled in the shallows as regards the blessings which ensue because of this. He is the Priest and Victim. On earth He died to save us and now He lives in heaven to keep us. *Since then we have a great high priest Who has passed through the heavens, Jesus, the Son of God, let us hold fast our confession. For we have not a high priest Who is unable to sympathise with our weaknesses, but One Who in every respect has been tempted as we, yet without sin. Let us then with confidence draw near to the throne of grace, that we may receive mercy and find grace to help in time of need* (Hebrews 4:14-16).

Jesus, my great high priest
Offered His blood and died
My guilty conscience seeks
No sacrifice beside
His powerful blood did once atone
And now it pleads before the throne.

CHAPTER THREE

The Fragrance Of The Sweetest Person

THE UNIQUE CHRISM : THE UNIQUE CHRIST

It is written of the fragrant anointing oil in Exodus 30:32:-
*you shall make no other like it in composition; it is holy, and
it shall be holy to you.* This is then followed by the stern
warning that *whoever compounds any like it or whoever puts
any of it on an outsider shall be cut off from his people.* The
fragrant oil was thus lovely, but exceedingly special, and not
to be trifled with or treated as though it were common oil. The
anointing oil was unique in itself and unique in its purpose.

The uniqueness of the anointing oil, leads us to consider
the uniqueness of the Anointed One, the Lord Jesus Christ.
Truly there is none like Him. *He is the holy One of God* (John
6:69), *His cheeks are beds of spices, yielding fragrance. His
lips are lilies, distilling liquid myrrh* (Song of Solomon 5:13).
He is the incomparable Christ, *distinguished among ten
thousand* (Song of Solomon 5:10).

Just as the anointing oil could not and was not to be
imitated, so likewise with Christ. Thus the Bible gives us the
warning to *Take heed that you are not led astray; for many*

will come in My name, saying "I am He!" (Luke 21:8). *For false Christs and false prophets will arise* (Matthew 24:24).

But just where does the uniqueness and incomparability of Christ lie? This we will consider now by considering the uniqueness of His:- Constitution, Conception, Character, Cleanliness, Cross, Conquest and Coming.

1. THE UNIQUENESS OF HIS CONSTITUTION

Christ is unique in His constitution in that He is the God-Man. He is fully human and yet fully Divine and yet one Person. It is a mystery as to how this can be so, but where reason cannot comprehend, faith bows in adoring worship. The Bible is crystal clear that *in Him the whole fullness of deity dwells bodily* (Colossians 2:10). Erroneous views concerning Christ mean an erroneous Christianity, thus in 421 AD, to combat heresy, the Council of Chalcedon was forced to define:-

"our Lord Jesus Christ is one and the same, that He is perfect in Godhead and perfect in manhood, truly God and truly man, ... in two natures, unconfusedly, immutably, indivisibly, inseparably..."

Take note that both the deity and humanity of Christ are an essential of the Christian Faith. If Christ were not God, His death would not have been an eternal sacrifice; if He were not Man, He could not have died for our sins to pay their terrible wages. Christ is unique in His constitution. He is the God-Man - 'our God contracted to a span, incomprehensibly made man.'

2. THE UNIQUENESS OF HIS CONCEPTION

The Lord Jesus Christ both entered and exited this world in a supernatural manner. He was born of a virgin, and thirty three years later ascended to heaven on a cloud. The Bible is plain to all except unbelief in asserting that Jesus Christ was 'conceived by the Holy Spirit, born of the Virgin Mary.' Scepticism as regards Christ's virgin birth has an ancient pedigree. Dr Luke records for us Mary's initial puzzlement *"How shall this be, since I have no husband?"* (Luke 1:34) and also the answer from heaven: *The Holy Spirit will come upon you, and the power of the Most High will overshadow you; therefore the child to be born will be called holy, the Son of God* (Luke 1:35).

The virgin birth of Christ is fundamental. God was Jesus's Father. Jesus is the eternally begotten Son of God - Bethlehem was not His beginning. This had to be, as a human father would mean a human failure. If Jesus were a mere son of Adam, He, like us, would have inherited Adam's sin, and so would be unable to redeem sinners. But as the Last Adam, Jesus was free from the corruption and pollution of sin, and thus able to offer up His life *without blemish to God* (Hebrews 9:14). Only a sinless one is qualified to redeem sinners. Every priest of Aaron's line was *bound to offer sacrifice for his own sins as well as for those of the people* (Hebrews 5:3), but *He has no need, like those high priests, to offer sacrifices daily, first for his own sins and then for those of the people; He did this once for all when He offered up Himself* (Hebrews 7:27). The virgin birth of Christ was an exact fulfilment of the prophecy of Isaiah made hundreds of years previously:- *Behold, a virgin shall conceive and bear a Son, and shall call His name Immanuel* (that is God is with us) (Isaiah 7:14).

3. THE UNIQUENESS OF HIS CHARACTER

How can we begin to describe the uniqueness of the character of the ever blessed Son of God, the loveliest Person to ever walk this earth? We will have to be selective. But we could consider this from the angle of His being: i. Unique in His Words ii. Unique in His Ways.

i. Unique in His Words

"No man ever spoke like this Man!" (John 7:46) reported the officers of the chief priests and pharisees - and they were right. Peter confessed to Jesus *"You have the words of eternal life"* (John 6:68). Jesus was unique in His words. *His word was with authority* (Luke 4:32). Who ever made such an affirmation as *All things have been delivered to Me by My Father; and no one knows the Son except the Father; and no one knows the Father except the Son and anyone to Whom the Son chooses to reveal Him* (Matthew 11:27)? Who, following on from such an affirmation, ever gave such an invitation as *Come to Me all who labour and are heavy laden and I will give you rest* (Matthew 11:28).

ii. Unique in His Ways

Jesus's character was manifest in His conduct. His ways were as marvellous as His words. Where do we begin? Jesus touched lepers and they were cleansed instantly. Jesus gave sight to the blind. Jesus calmed the stormy sea. Jesus spoke the word of forgiveness to sinners. He raised the dead. He healed the sick. He cared for the needy .... the list is exhaustless. John says *there are also many other things which Jesus did; were every one of them to be written, I suppose that the world itself could not contain the books that would be written* (John 21:25). Equally as marvellous is the transformation that Jesus makes in lives today! *If anyone is in Christ, he is a new creation; the old has passed away, behold the new has come* (2 Corinthians 5:17).

4. THE UNIQUENESS OF HIS CLEANLINESS

It takes a sinless one to redeem sinners. Jesus was unique among men in that He was totally, absolutely, and immaculately morally pure in His heart and life. He was free from the moral pollution of sin, totally sinless by nature and practice. He Himself had the seeming audacity to challenge *Which of you convicts Me of sin?* (John 8:46) to which the writer to the Hebrews concurs. Yes, Jesus knows what it is like to be human, he writes, thus He can sympathise with our weakness-but He is adamant that Jesus was *without sin* (Hebrews 4:15)- *holy, blameless, unstained, separated from sinners* (Hebrews 7:26). It is the sinlessness of Christ which gives efficacy to His cross. The Passover instructions were unmistakable - *Your lamb shall be without blemish* (Exodus 12:5). Peter, who knew the Lord at close quarters, knew Him to be *like that of a lamb without blemish or spot* (1 Peter 1:19). Which leads us logically to:-

5. THE UNIQUENESS OF HIS CROSS

The saying is sure and worthy of full acceptance, that Christ Jesus came into the world to save sinners (1 Timothy 1:15) - and He did so by dying the cruel death of the cross. Jesus was born to die. He achieved much in His life, but, and we say it reverently, He accomplished far more by His death. His death avails for all time as an eternal sacrifice for sin. Crucifixion was common in those cruel Roman times - but this One Who died by crucifixion was uncommon and unparalleled. The centurion standing by realised this. Mark recorded *when the centurion, who stood facing Him, saw that He thus breathed His last, he said, "Truly this Man was the Son of God"* (Mark 15:39).

It is the worth of Christ that affects His work. His character and constitution affect His cross. It was a unique event with unique effects. *He has appeared once for all at the end of the age to put away sin by the sacrifice of Himself* (Hebrews 9:26). *Christ also died for sins once for all, the righteous for the unrighteous, that He might bring us to God* (1 Peter 3:18).

The power of the Cross may still be experienced and seen at work even today. Sinners, aware of their need, plight and the burden of their sin, may kneel in penitent faith at its foot and receive instant salvation! Yet even those who have trusted the crucified Saviour for many years can never meditate on the cross and its finished Work too much:-

To Calvary, Lord, in spirit now
our weary souls repair
To dwell upon Thy dying love
and taste its sweetness there

Sweet resting place of every heart
that feels the plague of sin
Yet knows that deep mysterious joy
the peace of God within.

The cross was not the end however, thus we turn to:-

6. THE UNIQUENESS OF HIS CONQUEST

Jesus Christ is unique and peerless in that He conquered the grave. In overcoming death He defeated the king of terrors and terror of kings. Jesus began His life in a virgin womb, and it seemed that He would end His life in a virgin tomb, but this was not to be.

The earliest Christian creed affirms *He was raised on the third day in accordance with the Scriptures* (1 Corinthians 15:4). Peter likewise, during his first sermon, proclaimed the resurrection of Jesus Christ from the dead - for "*God raised Him up, having loosed the pangs of death, because it was not possible for Him to be held by it*" (Acts 2:24).

The Christian Faith rests on the rock of Christ's resurrection. It is surely the most attested fact of history, indisputable to all except those blind to the evidence, determined not to believe. Christ's resurrection proves that He is the eternal Son of God; *He was designated Son of God in power according to the Spirit of holiness by His resurrection from the dead* (Romans 1:4). Christ's resurrection proves that our sins are forgiven. It is God's divine seal of approval on Him Who gave His life as an atoning sacrifice on Calvary's cross - *Who was put to death for our trespasses and raised for our justification* (Romans 4:25). Christ's resurrection proves that one day, all who trust in Him will have a glorious spiritual body, just like His, *Christ has been raised from the dead, the first fruits of those who have fallen asleep* (1 Corinthians 15:20).

The empty tomb and the risen Christ show that death is a defeated and vanquished foe; and the best is, that one day the victory of Christ will be ours as well:- *When the perishable puts on the imperishable, and the mortal puts on immortality, then shall come to pass the saying that is written, "Death is swallowed up in victory." "O death, where is thy victory? O death, where is thy sting?"* (1 Corinthians 15:54,55).

> *Oh, joyful day, oh glorious hour*
> *When Jesus by Almighty power*
> *Revived and left the grave!*
> *In all His works behold Him great*
> *Before Almighty to create*
> *Almighty now to save!*

6. THE UNIQUENESS OF HIS COMING

The second coming of Christ will be an event both unique, unsurpassed and unsurpassable. Christ's second coming will be the climax, culmination and consummation of God's redemptive purposes, and it will bring in *the new heavens and a new earth in which righteousness dwells* (2 Peter 3:13).

What a day it will be when all *will see the Son of Man coming in clouds with great power and glory* (Mark 13:26) - and what a contrast to His first coming in humiliation and relative obscurity. *Behold, He is coming with the clouds and every eye will see Him* (Revelation 1:7). The head that once was crowned with thorns will then come to reign! Revelation tells us with prophetic foresight *on His head are many diadems ... He has a name inscribed, King of kings and Lord of lords* (Revelation 19:12,16).

Jesus is coming again! At His first coming, He was mocked, blasphemed, spat upon, and treated with the contempt which eventually nailed Him to a cross on a public thoroughfare. The day is drawing near however when the roles will be reversed. *For He must reign until He has put all His enemies under His feet* (1 Corinthians 15:25). ... *that at the Name of Jesus every knee should bow, in heaven and on earth and under the earth, and every tongue confess that Jesus Christ is Lord to the glory of God the Father* (Philippians 2:10,11).

And so we see something of the uniqueness of Christ, the Name above all names. He is unique in His conception, character and conduct. He is unique as regards His constitution, cross and conquest. At His second coming His uniqueness will be vindicated beyond all doubt to all. Jesus alone is worthy of our praise.

> *O, could I speak the matchless worth*
> *O, could I sound the glories forth*
> *Which in my Saviour shine!*
> *I'd soar and touch the heavenly strings*
> *And vie with Gabriel while he sings*
> *In notes almost divine.*

CHAPTER FOUR

The Fragrance Of The
Supplicant's Prayers

*And the Lord said to Moses, "Take sweet spices, stacte,
and onycha and galbanum, sweet spices with pure
frankincense (of each shall there be an equal part), and
make an incense blended as by the perfumer ... And the
incense which you shall make according to its composition, you shall make for yourselves; it shall be to you holy
to the Lord. Whoever makes any like it to use as perfume
shall be cut off from his people*
(Exodus 30:34-38).

Here then, we have another recipe for a special, unique and
literally heavenly fragrance, namely the sweetest smelling
incense which Aaron and his sons were to burn as a *perpetual
incense before the Lord through your generations* (Exodus
30:7). God's instructions were strict and clear - and so Bezalel
obeyed and *He made the holy anointing oil also, and the pure
fragrant   incense, blended as by the perfumer* (Exodus
37:29).

1. THE PERFUMED PRAYER

Incense in the Bible is often a symbol for prayer. Such a
symbol is easily understood, if we imagine the incense being

burned on the golden altar, and its fragrant smoke ascending like prayer to heaven. Perhaps it was with this in mind that David wrote:- *I call upon Thee, O Lord; make haste to me! Give ear to my voice, when I call Thee! Let my prayer be counted as <u>incense</u> before Thee, and the lifting up of my hands an evening sacrifice* (Psalm 141:1,2). The perfumed smoke of the incense ascended heavenwards - *and the smoke of the incense rose with the prayers of the saints from the hand of the angel before God* (Revelation 8:4).

God is in heaven, but the wonder is, that our feeble prayers ascend to Him and reach His ears! *In my distress I called upon the Lord; to my God I cried for help. From His temple He heard my voice, and my cry to Him reached His ears* (Psalm 18:6).

There is a perfume to prayer. God delights to hear His children pray and come before Him in childlike dependence and trust.

> *Much incense is ascending*
> *Before the eternal throne*
> *God graciously is bending*
> *To hear each feeble groan*
> *To all our prayers and praises*
> *Christ adds His sweet perfume*
> *And love the censer raises*
> *Their odours to consume*

2. THE PEERLESS PRAYER

i. His Heavenly Petitions

We quoted above that the incense was *a perpetual incense before the Lord through your generations* (Exodus 30:7). What a picture this is of the prayer-full Christ, Who constantly intercedes for His Own! Jesus, our great high priest *holds His priesthood permanently, because He continues for ever. Consequently He is able for all time to save those who draw near to God through Him, since He always lives to make intercession for them* (Hebrews 7:24,25). Put those two verses, over a thousand years apart, side by side:- *a perpetual incense throughout your generations* (Exodus 30:7) and *He always lives to make intercession for them* (Hebrews 7:25). What a comfort it is amidst our feeble prayer life, to know that Jesus is in heaven praying for us right now! *Who is at the right hand of God, Who indeed intercedes for us* (Romans 8:34). Yet *we have not a high priest Who is unable to sympathise with our weaknesses but One Who in every respect has been tempted as we are, yet without sin* (Hebrews 4:15).

Our High Priest is a supplicating High Priest : Our High Priest is a sympathetic High Priest - He lived in a real, flesh and blood body and walked this sin-scarred earth in the land of Israel two thousand years ago. He is characterised by prayer for us now - but equally so, when He graced this earth, His life was characterised by prayer:-

ii. His Earthly Prayers

Jesus life on earth was indeed marked by prayer. This shows that Jesus was truly human as well as truly divine. Prayer betrays humanity, as what is prayer but an acknowledgement of a total dependence upon God?

Our Saviour here, as the Perfect Man, is an example for us to emulate. At the outset of His ministry *when Jesus also had been baptised and was praying, the heaven was opened* (Luke 3:21) - do we begin our new ventures with prayer? Mark informs us of Jesus' regular habit - *in the morning, a great while before day, He rose and went out to a lonely place, and there He prayed* (Mark 1:35) - and how can we afford to begin the day any differently? Then what of the important decisions and choices of our lives? We know how Jesus faced these. *He went out to the mountain to <u>pray</u>, and all night He continued in prayer to God. And when it was day, He called His disciples, and chose from them twelve ...* (Luke 6:12,13).

In his 'agony at Gethsemene,' *Jesus offered up <u>prayers and supplications</u>, with loud cries and tears, to Him Who was able to save Him from death, and He was heard for His godly fear* (Hebrews 5:7). We can be encouraged to do the same in our lesser distresses. God says *Call upon Me in the day of trouble; I will deliver you, and you shall glorify Me* (Psalm 50:15).

The end of Jesus's earthly life was the incarnation of serenity. He prayed *Father into Thy hand I commit My spirit* (Luke 23:46). Oh that we could so do - and we can if we are Christ's! Because of Jesus, death is a conquered enemy. He has taken away its sting. And so we see something of the prominence of prayer in Jesus's earthly life.

3. THE PERSONAL PRAYER

Jesus once made the stupendous claim concerning His personal relationship to His Father *I always do what is pleasing to Him* (John 8:29). This would have been the height of audacity if the Father Himself had not said earlier *This is My beloved Son, with Whom I am well pleased* (Matthew 3:17). Alas, we know only too well of our imperfect prayer life, *If I had cherished iniquity in My heart, the Lord would not have listened* (Psalm 66:18). Sin, even in the believer, can block the channel to heaven - but such could never be the case with the sinless Christ. Thus we read *And Jesus lifted up His eyes and said "Father, I thank Thee that Thou hast heard Me. I knew that Thou hearest Me always ..."* (John 11:41,42).

We can be infinitely grateful that Jesus's prayers are always heard. Before He went to the cross He prayed for us.

Father, I desire that they also, whom Thou hast given Me, may be with Me where I am, to behold My glory which Thou hast given Me in Thy love for Me before the foundation of the world (John 17:24). There is a sense in which by going on to die at Calvary, Jesus answered His Own prayer. What confidence we may enjoy therefore because of the atoning sacrifice and the earthly and heavenly intercession of our Saviour.

> *His sweet atoning sacrifice*
> *Gives sanction to His claim*
> *Father, I will that all My saints*
> *Be with Me where I am*
>
> *Eternal life, at His request*
> *To every saint is given*
> *Safety on earth, and after death*
> *The plenitude of heaven*

4. THE POSSIBILITY OF PRAYER

The immense blessing of true Christian prayer just would not be possible apart from Christ. The Bible emphasises that prayer is always in the Name of Jesus. For example *Truly, truly, I say to you, if you ask anything of the Father, He will give it to you in My name. Hitherto you have asked nothing in My name; ask and you will receive, that your joy may be full* (John 16:23,24).

It is Jesus Who makes it possible for us to draw near to God in prayer. He makes it possible by i. His Sacrifice ii. His Spirit.

i. By His Sacrifice

It is a basic Christian axiom that Christ's death atoned for our sins - the sins which separated us from God. What an infinite difference there is between us before and after we got saved! *But now in Christ Jesus you who once were far off have been brought near in the blood of Christ* (Ephesians 3:13). The first fact which we notice about Paul after his conversion is *behold, He is praying* (Acts 9:11). It is the atoning blood of Jesus which enables the sinner to draw near to God. Thus, after extolling the virtues of Christ's atoning sacrifice in no uncertain terms, the writer of the Hebrews explains the glorious consequence :- *Therefore, brethren ... we have confidence to enter the sanctuary by the blood of Jesus ...* (Hebrews 10:19) - and it is true!

> *Behold the throne of grace - the promise calls us near*
> *There Jesus shows a smiling face - and waits to answer*
> *prayer*
> *That rich atoning blood, which sprinkled round I see*
> *Provides for those who come to God an all-prevailing*
> *plea.*

The sacrifice of Jesus makes prayer possible, but prayer is also made possible:-

ii. By His Spirit

How powerless our prayers would be if we prayed only in the unaided power of the flesh. Thankfully, we are promised and given the aid of God's Holy Spirit here, and so exhorted to *Pray at all times in the Spirit with all prayer and supplication* (Ephesians 6:18). *The Spirit helps us in our weakness; for we do not know how to pray as we ought, but the Spirit Himself intercedes for us with sighs too deep for words.... the Spirit intercedes for the saints according to the will of God* (Romans 8:26,27).

A. THE WONDER OF PRAYER'S ACCESSIBILITY

We must never lose sight of the wonder of prayer! Because of Jesus, the Almighty God is accessible. If we are

Christ's we are on intimate speaking terms with none other than Almighty God - *for through Him we have access in one Spirit to the Father* (Ephesians 2:18). Furthermore, because of Christ, our prayers are not only accessible but acceptable:-

B. THE WONDER OF PRAYER'S ACCEPTABILITY

When we pray, how can we be sure that our words are acceptable to God? If we know anything of our own hearts, we know that everything we do, prayer included, is tainted by sin and mixed and impure in its motive. Does the incense of our prayers really rise to heaven therefore? How could it possibly do so, we may wonder. We may take heart from the following 'perfumed text' of the Bible. *And another angel came and stood at the altar with a golden censer; and he was given much incense to mingle with the prayers of all the saints upon the golden altar before the throne; and the smoke of the incense rose with the prayers of the saints from the hand of the angel before God* (Revelation 8:3,4):-

"The angel is neither a mediator nor an intercessor. He does not bring his own offering but is given "much incense" and this symbol 'represents the intercession of Christ for His Church, which adds power and efficacy to the prayers of the Church'(Lenski). For it is only as the prayers of the saints are purified by Christ's intercession that they ascend to God as a fragrant offering." (G.B. Wilson)

Thus, because of Christ, our prayers are acceptable - *acceptable to God through Jesus Christ* (1 Peter 2:5).

Gathering up these precious truths:-

> *No prayer is made on earth alone*
> *The Holy Spirit pleads*
> *And Jesus on the eternal throne*
> *For sinners intercedes*

5. THE PERFECT PRAYER

Jesus's prayer life was awesome. So much was this so, that on one occasion *He was praying in a certain place, and when He had ceased, one of His disciples said to Him, "Lord, teach us to pray..."* (Luke 11:1). Jesus graciously answered this request, and in doing so He bequeathed to us the perfect prayer. It is commonly known as 'the Lord's Prayer,' - but more correctly it is 'The Disciple's Prayer.' In this perfect prayer, Luke gathers up for us all the essentials of prayer in just three verses. *"When you pray say:*

"Father, hallowed by Thy name
Thy kingdom come
Give us each day our daily bread
and forgive us our sins, for we ourselves forgive
every one who is indebted to us;
and lead us not into temptation"(Luke 11:2-4).

This prayer has a beautiful symmetry, beginning with God and His glory, and then turning to ourselves and our needs:-

GOD AND HIS GLORY

The prayer begins with <u>adoption</u>. *Father*. This is our highest blessing; through Christ we are children of God by adoption and grace. *And because you are sons, God has sent the Spirit of His Son into our hearts crying "Abba! Father"* (Galatians 4:6).

The prayer continues with <u>adoration</u>. *hallowed be Thy name*. God is our Father, but He is indeed in heaven and He is indeed holy. May we too thus fear and revere Him, and be zealous for His honour *for the Lord our God is holy* (Psalm 99:9).

The prayer for God's glory closes with <u>anticipation</u>, *Thy kingdom come* and as Matthew amplifies *Thy will be done on earth as it is in heaven.* Do we then long and pray for the coming of God's kingdom? What a day it will be *for the earth will be filled with the knowledge of the glory of the Lord as the waters cover the sea* (Isaiah 11:9). We, of course, cannot bring in God's eternal kingdom; but if His kingdom entails His will being done, we can pray "Thy will be done Lord, and let it be done in me."

WE AND OUR WANTS

We pray for provision. *Give us each day our daily bread.* We are totally dependent on God for the bread of this world and the bread of life. Even in our lean years we may ask and receive from God, just like Israel in the barren wilderness. *They asked, and He ... gave them bread from heaven in abundance* (Psalm 105:40).

We pray for pardon *and forgive us our sins, for we ourselves forgive everyone who is indebted to us.* Alas, we always need God's pardon. John, writing to Christians penned the obvious truth:- *if we say we have no sin we deceive ourselves and the truth is not in us* but then continued on a happier note, *If we confess our sins He is faithful and just and will forgive our sins and cleanse us from all unrighteousness* (1 John 1:8,9). Sin is an infinite debt to God; but in Christ He has graciously cleared our debt! This being so, how can we not forgive others their lesser debts against us? (See Matthew 18:23 ff). *As the Lord has forgiven you, so you must also forgive* (Colossians 3:13) - and who says Christianity is an opium?

We pray for protection *and lead us not into temptation.* How weak we are and prone to fall. Yet He *is able to keep you from falling* (Jude 24). Matthew expands this somewhat with the petition *but deliver us from the evil one.* It is a reminder that *Your adversary the devil prowls around like a roaring lion, seeking some one to devour* (1 Peter 5:8). And so our Lord concludes the perfect prayer as regards our own needs - *My God will supply every need of yours according to His riches in glory in Christ Jesus* (Philippians 4:19).

THE IMPLICIT TRINITY

It is interesting to note the Trinitarian nature of the perfect prayer, which may have become blunt through familiarity:-

1. Give us this day our daily bread - it is God the Father Who provides for the daily needs of His children.

2. And forgive us our sins - it is only the death of Jesus, God's Son, which meets this need.

3. And lead us not into temptation - it is only by the power of the Holy Spirit that we are enabled to resist evil, for *He Who is in you is greater than he who is in the world* (1 John 4:4).

THE CLOSING DOXOLOGY

Fittingly, the early church added an appropriate ending to this perfect prayer - *For Thine is the kingdom and the power and the glory, for ever*, - to which we can only add our *Amen!* and pray *Lord, teach us to pray.*

Lord teach us how to pray aright
With reverence and with fear
Though dust and ashes in Thy sight
We may, we must draw near

We perish if we cease from prayer
O grant us power to pray!
And when to meet Thee we prepare
Lord, meet us by the way.

CHAPTER FIVE

The Fragrance Of The Saline Promise

Make an incense blended as by the perfumer,
seasoned with salt, pure and holy
(Exodus 30:35).

The sacred and special incense which Aaron and his sons were to burn, gives us many illustrations, if we dig below the surface, of Christ and His benefits to us. You will have noticed above, that one of its special ingredients was *salt*.

Salt is a universal and common substance, and, as is often the case, the Bible takes up this natural object and gives it a supernatural significance.

We see this transignificance of the ordinary in the life of our Saviour. He described Himself, amongst other things as *Bread* (John 6:35), *Light* (John 8:12) and *Water* (John 4:14).

God graciously accommodates to our humanity, and uses the physical to illustrate the spiritual. He meets us where we are and takes us on to higher matters. This is so concerning salt - as we shall see:-

1. THE SALT OF THE COVENANT

The Covenant concept is part of the very warp and woof of the Bible, which is divided into two, the Old Covenant and the New Covenant. The 'Covenant' refers to the binding bond which God lovingly makes between Himself and His people. It is always a covenant of grace. In His sovereign love, God calls a people to Himself and says *I will be your God and they shall be My people* (Jeremiah 31:33). The initiative in the covenant is always with God. It is He Who chooses and calls a people to Himself. It is He Who loves with an eternal love that will not let us go. *I plighted My troth to you and entered into a covenant with you, says the Lord God, and you became Mine* (Ezekiel 16:8).

Salt was a sign of God's covenant with His Old Testament people. The Divine instructions to Moses at Sinai included these:- *You shall season all your cereal offerings with salt; you shall not let the salt of the covenant with your God be lacking from your cereal offering; with all your offerings you shall offer salt* (Leviticus 2:13). A little later on, God likewise reminded Israel again of *a covenant of salt for ever before the Lord for you and for your offspring with you* (Numbers 18:19):-

Salt "was often used among Oriental peoples for ratifying agreements, so that salt became the symbol of fidelity and constancy. In the Levitical cereal offerings, salt was used as a preservative to typify the eternal nature of the 'covenant of salt' existing between God and Israel." (NEW BIBLE DICTIONARY, I.V.P., 1982, p.1056).

"The partaking of salt by different persons together is regarded among the Arabs as a pledge of friendship. ... By using salt in their sacrifices the people were bound to Jehovah in most solemn covenant." (MANNERS AND CUSTOMS OF THE BIBLE, James M. Freeman, Bridge Publishing, 1972, p.86).

2. THE SALT OF THE CHRIST

It is written of Christ *He is the mediator of a new covenant* (Hebrews 9:15). He is indeed, and this new covenant between God and His people was sealed with nothing less than Christ's Own life blood. Jesus said *This is My blood of the new covenant which is poured out for many for the forgiveness of sins* (Matthew 26:28). Jesus's blood is the fulfilment of God's new covenant promise in Jeremiah 31, where the Lord said *I will make a new covenant with the house of Israel and the house of Judah ... for I will forgive their iniquity, and I will remember their sin no more.* It is the forgiving blood of Jesus which establishes God's covenant and makes us His people - a holy God just cannot have fellowship with an unforgiven people. The salt of God's forgiveness in Christ gives savour and flavour. Life without Christ is insipid indeed - death without Christ is even worse.

Jesus said of His new covenant people *You are the salt of the earth* (Matthew 5:13), and whilst it is not explicit, it is implicit that what is to be true of the Christian was actually true of the Christ:-

i. The salt of His purity

Salt is a pure substance, and was used in Biblical times to purify. New born babies were thus *washed with water... rubbed with salt* (Ezekiel 16:4). Salt thus speaks to us of the immaculate purity of Christ. He alone was unique among men in that He was free from every taint of sin. All of us are sinners by nature and practice. Christians are saved sinners - but sinners nevertheless, and some of the thoughts that creep into our minds are so impure that we blush with shame in the cold light of day.

Jesus was characterised by total and absolute purity in all of His thoughts, words, deeds, manners and motives. The sinlessness of Christ is a Christian fundamental, as only a sinless one is qualified to be the Saviour of sinners. It was said of Jesus *This Man receives sinners and eats with them* (Luke 15:2). Yet Jesus Himself, although mixing with sinners, remained Himself untouched and untainted by the pollution of sin. He is indeed *holy, blameless, unstained, separated from sinners, exalted above the heavens* (Hebrews 7:26).

Peter and John were two of Jesus's closest earthly friends. They lived with Him at close quarters. Yet John testified *in Him there is no sin* (1 John 3:5) and Peter likewise *He committed no sin, no guile was found on His lips* (1 Peter 2:22). Salt reminds us of Christ's purity. But consider too:-

ii. The salt of His incorruptibility

Before the days of canning and the deep freeze, salt was rubbed into food to prevent its decaying. Food soon went rotten and inedible in the hot middle east if it was not preserved by salting or drying.

A consequence of sin is death and decay. *Sin when it is full grown brings forth death* (James 1:15). Poor Martha thus said of her dead brother whose body was lying dead in a tomb *Lord, by this time there will be an odour, for he has been dead for four days* (John 11:39). The sinless Christ was not subject to the law of death and decay. This is supremely seen in His bodily resurrection from the dead on the third day. The triumph of Christ over death and sin is the supreme vindication of both Himself and His claims. The incorruptibility of the One characterised by incomparability, as evidenced by His resurrection, was Peter's theme on the day of Pentecost when he preached to the crowds:- *Jesus of Nazareth ...David says concerning Him ... For Thou wilt not abandon My soul to Hades, nor let Thy Holy One see corruption ... David ..*

foresaw and spoke of the resurrection of Christ, that He was
not abandoned to Hades, nor did His flesh see corruption
(Acts 2:22,25,27,31).

What was wonderfully true of the incorruptible Christ will
be wonderfully true of the Christian, in time. The full-orbed
Christian hope is the resurrection of the body on the Last Day.
*What is sown is perishable, what is raised is imperishable ...
When the perishable puts on the imperishable, and the mortal
puts on immortality, then shall come to pass the saying that
is written "Death is swallowed up in victory"* (1 Corinthians
15:42,54). We will then know in full what we already claim
to know, that *God so loved the world that He gave His only
Son that whoever believes in Him should not <u>perish</u> but have
eternal life* (John 3:16). The salt of God's covenant in Christ
keeps and will keep us from perishing eternally.

iii. The salt of His thirsty

Salt, or rather, too much salt, can upset our bodies' water
balance and make us thirsty. Salt thus paradoxically is a bane
as well as a blessing. Salt can give us a raging thirst that just
has to be quenched.

Before we come to Christ, God may see fit to give us a
raging spiritual thirst. Circumstances and crises ordained by
Him may give us a thirst for reality - a thirst which the passing
baubles, bubbles and trinkets of this world are unable to
quench. This world is deceptive. It gives us a thirst which it
cannot quench. Unless we see that only God Himself can
quench our thirst, the things and pursuits of this world are an
addiction which lead to spiritual death. We may apply Jesus's
words to those who constantly seek to draw water from the
well of this world:- *Everyone who drinks of this water will
thirst again* (John 4:13). Contrast this though with the water
that He gives:- *but whoever drinks of the water that I shall give*

Him will never thirst; the water that I shall give him will become in him a spring of water, welling up to eternal life (John 4:14).

3. THE SALT OF THE CHRISTIAN

i. The Christian's Savour (Our Taste)

Let us return to the words of Jesus quoted earlier, but let us quote them in full. *You are the salt of the earth; but if the salt has lost its taste, how shall its saltness be restored? It is no longer good for anything except to be thrown out and trodden under foot by men* (Matthew 5:13). Tasteless salt is a contradiction in terms, like a dark light or a square circle! We may interpret this exhortation of Jesus by gathering up some of the thoughts we have considered so far:-

If we are Christians we are *the salt of the earth*. We are salt and we are to be salt. We are the covenant people of God; He is irrevocably committed to us, as we should be to Him in love and faithfulness - but does our behaviour and life and manner betray that this is so? Then, as Christians we are to be pure. Christ indeed *gave Himself for us to ... purify for Himself a people of His Own* ... (Titus 2:14). James's definition of *Religion that is pure and undefiled before God* included the command to *keep oneself unstained from the world* (James 1:27). Christ made us pure when He washed us in His precious blood. Nevertheless, we are to be pure and faithful to God - *Blessed are the pure in heart for they shall see God* (Matthew 5:8). But are we such? Do we allow the moral pollution of the world to taint us by the company we keep, the papers we read and the TV we watch? Do we have a purifying effect on those around us, or do we shamefully add to the pollution?

ii. The Christian's Speech (Our Talk)

What comes out of our mouths? The tongue, in many respects, is the barometer of the kind of person we are. Jesus once said *out of the abundance of the heart the mouth speaks* (Luke 6:45). Paul gives us the exhortation *Let your speech always be gracious, seasoned with salt* (Colossians 4:6). But is it? How we need the help of God's Holy Spirit. Christ commands us to be salt. Would He ever give us a command we could not fulfil? No. *His commandments are not burdensome* (1 John 5:3). With the commandment He gives the enablement! He desires the very best for us and the uttermost glory for God the Father. Obeying Christ is the only way of true happiness. Let us then re-commit ourselves afresh to Him in covenant-love, obeying Him Who said *My yoke is easy and My burden is light* (Matthew 11:30). *And I am sure that He Who began a good work in you will bring it to completion at the day of Jesus Christ* (Philippians 1:6).

> *The work which His goodness began*
> *The arm of His strength will complete*
> *His promise is Yea and Amen*
> *And never was forfeited yet*
> *Things future, nor things that are now*
> *Not all things below nor above*
> *Can make Him His purpose forego*
> *Or sever my soul from His love*

CHAPTER SIX

The Fragrance Of The Saved Priesthood

(The Priesthood of all Believers)

And you shall anoint Aaron and his sons, and consecrate them, that they may serve Me as priests
(Exodus 30:30).

THE SEPARATE PRIESTLY CASTE

It is both interesting and revealing to trace the concept of priesthood right through the Bible:- In Old Testament times the priesthood was limited to a special 'caste,' namely, as our verse tells us, to Aaron and his sons. Priests were thus born not made - and anyone who attempted to usurp the prerogative of the priesthood strictly limited to Aaron's line, soon felt the wrath of God against him in judgement. This knew no favourites. In 2 Chronicles 26 we read of King Uzziah who took it upon himself to act as priest. Immediately *leprosy broke out on his forehead, in the presence of the priests in the house of the Lord ... And King Uzziah was a leper to the day of his death, and being a leper dwelt in a separate house, for he was excluded from the house of the Lord* (17,21).

THE SUPERLATIVE PRIESTLY CHRIST

With the coming of Christ in the fullness of time, the whole temple structure along with its sacrificial system was brought to an end. Christ fulfilled it all. *For Christ is the end of the law that everyone who has faith may be justified* (Romans 10:4). *Truly something greater than the temple is here* (Matthew 12:6).

Christ brought an end to the continuous blood sacrifice of the temple. *He has no need, like those high priests, to offer sacrifices daily first for his own sins and those of the people; He did this once for all when He offered up Himself* (Hebrews 7:27).

THE SAINTS' PRIESTLY CONDITION

Christ indeed abolished the priesthood in the sense of having a special caste of people who offer sacrifice to God. Yet, paradoxically, the priesthood did not end with the coming of Christ. According to the New Testament every believer is a priest! *You have been anointed by the Holy One* (1 John 2:20) wrote John to his fellow believers. All believers have thus, been anointed with the fragrant oil, and now have the unique privilege of serving God and their fellow men in the capacity of priests.

The 'Priesthood of all Believers' is a precious but neglected New Testament truth. It was a truth which was recovered at the time of the Protestant Reformation in the 16th century - before then it had been largely lost. The Roman Catholic church taught, and still teaches, that only a certain category of person (a single, 'ordained' male) can act as 'priest' and offer the 'sacrifice of the Mass.' Such teaching is foreign to the New Testament, and a retrograde step back into the Old Testament shadows - not to mention a blasphemous undoing and undermining of the completed Calvary Work of Christ.

The Gospel is a great leveller and equaliser. A Christian is one who realised his/her lost condition and fled to Christ. All Christians are saved not by their own merits and efforts, but by the sheer grace of God in Christ. There can be no separate class here. Boasting is excluded. None is too bad to be beyond redemption. None is too good not to need redeeming. Thus all Christians are equal in status. There may be differences in role and function, according to Divine gifts bestowed, but all are equal in the sight of the Lord, *For there is no distinction between Jew and Greek; the same Lord is Lord of all and bestows His riches upon all who call upon Him. For "every one who calls upon the name of the Lord will be saved"* (Romans 10:12,13).

Let us now consider the priesthood of the New Testament - *our* priesthood if we are Christians. As priests it is evident that we have a special Status, Sacrifice, Supplication, Sharing and Service - as we will now see:-

A. OUR STATUS AS PRIESTS

The Apostle Peter, writing to his fellow Christians reminded them *you are a chosen race, a <u>royal priesthood</u>, a holy nation, God's Own people, that you may declare the wonderful deeds of Him Who called you out of darkness into His marvellous light. Once you were no people, but now you are God's people; once you had not received mercy but now you have received mercy* (1 Peter 2:9,10). A few verses earlier Peter had also reminded them of their calling *to be a holy <u>priesthood</u>, to offer spiritual sacrifices acceptable to God through Jesus Christ* (1 Peter 2:5). These verses show that all believers are priests. All believers stand in a special, chosen, called, cleansed and Covenantal relationship with Almighty

God - a covenant relationship which time and eternity cannot and will not break. The Church therefore is the fulfilment and completion of God's promise to His Old Testament community to whom God has said at Sinai *you shall be to Me a kingdom of priests and a holy nation* (Exodus 19:6). The wonder of this will never grow old, even in heaven! Heaven's clear cry is the same *To Him Who loves us and has freed us from our sins by His blood, and made us a kingdom, priests to His God and Father* (Revelation 1:5,6). *Thou wast slain and by Thy blood didst ransom men for God ... and hast made them a kingdom and priests to our God* (Revelation 5:9,10). Isaiah prophesied *You shall be called priests of the Lord* (Isaiah 61:6) - and so we are! The priests had a special relationship and access to God, and by virtue of His Son, so now does every Christian. *Since we have a great High Priest... let us draw near to the throne of grace ...* (Hebrews 4:14). *We have confidence to enter the sanctuary by the blood of Jesus* (Hebrews 10:19).

> *So near so very near to God*
> *Nearer I cannot be*
> *for in the Person of His Son*
> *I am as near as He*

B. OUR SACRIFICE AS PRIESTS

In Old Testament times sacrifice was undertaken to procure salvation. In New Testament times sacrifice is undertaken *because* of salvation - but, of course, it is sacrifice of a different kind. The sacrifice undertaken now is the sacrifice of gratitude to God for providing His Son to be the perfect atonement for sin. Salvation is all of grace. Service is all of gratitude. Salvation is the result of Divine sacrifice. Service is the response of human sacrifice. This latter is a sacrifice of life and lip, walk and talk. The classic expression of this is Romans 12:1. Having spent eleven chapters unfolding and extolling the mercies of God and His justifying grace, Paul characteristically pens one of his great 'therefores.' *I appeal to you therefore, brethren, by the mercies of God, to present your bodies as a living sacrifice, holy and acceptable to God, which is your spiritual worship.* Here we have the living sacrifice of a life in grateful response to God's mercies received - and can we offer anything less? *He did not spare His only Son but gave Him up for us all* (Romans 8:32).

Similarly, the sacrifice of the lips occurs at the end of a letter extolling the wonders of Christ's sacrifice. Hebrews opens with Christ's sacrifice - *when He had made purification for sins, He sat down at the right hand of the Majesty on High* (Hebrews 1:3). Hebrews closes with *Through Him then let us continually offer up a sacrifice of praise to God, that is, the fruit of lips that acknowledge His name* (Hebrews 13:15) - and when we have been enthralled with the work of Christ for us, as extolled in the pages of Hebrews, we know that we have every reason to offer such a sacrifice of praise. Worship is the highest activity of heaven and earth. How much more reason than the Psalmist, having received the light we have, have we to *Ascribe to the Lord the glory due to His name; bring an offering, and come into His courts* (Psalm 96:8).

C. OUR SUPPLICATION AS PRIESTS

We should never lose sight of the wonder of what we are doing when we pray. As a priest had special access to God, so now does every Christian. Amazingly, every Christian is on speaking terms with the God of gods! This access is another fruit of the sacrifice of Christ - *for through Him we both have access in one Spirit to the Father* (Ephesians 2:18). At its basic level, prayer is simply 'talking to God,' bringing to Him our needs and 'spreading out our helplessness' before Him. We ignore Christ's encouragements to pray at our peril. It seems from the New Testament that God is always keener to listen to us than we are to pray to Him. Jesus said *Ask and it will be given you; seek and you will find; knock and it will be opened to you. For everyone who asks receives, and he who seeks finds and to him who knocks it will be opened* (Matthew 7:7-8). Then note his gentle rebuke in the following contrast *Or what man of you, if his son asks for bread, will give him a stone? Or if he asks for a fish, will give him a serpent? If you then, who are evil, know how to give good gifts to your children, how much more will your Father Who is in heaven give good things to those who ask Him!* (Matthew 7:9-11). We are thus encouraged to lift our own needs before the throne of grace, as well as the needs of others. *Let my prayer be counted as incense before Thee, and the lifting up of my hands as an evening sacrifice!* (Psalm 141:2).

You will notice from Exodus 28 and 39, that Aaron, the original high priest, literally bore the names of each of the twelve tribes of Israel engraved in stone upon his heart before the Lord. *So Aaron shall bear the names of the sons of Israel in the breastpiece of judgement upon his heart, when he goes into the holy place, to bring them to continual remembrance before the Lord* (Exodus 28:29). In the first instance we apply this to Christ our great High Priest. He also most blessedly bears our names upon His heart before the Father. But a second application concerns ourselves and our status as priests. As we are now priests, we may bring the names of those on our heart before God - and if we know what real prayer is, isn't this the very best we can do for anyone?

D. OUR SHARING AS PRIESTS

Paul's happy letter to the Philippians was written from a Roman prison cell, to express his thanks to the believers in

Philippi for a gift which they had sent him - a gift in season which made his life more comfortable. Interestingly, their giving is described as *a fragrant offering*. Wrote Paul, *I am filled, having received from Epaphroditus the gifts you sent, a fragrant offering, a sacrifice acceptable and pleasing to God* (Philippians 4:18).

What a privilege and blessing it is thus to help and support those who serve God. Giving to them, unusual as it sounds is *a sacrifice acceptable and pleasing to God*. Hebrews 13:16 likewise states *Do not neglect to do good and to share what you have, for such sacrifices are pleasing to God.* We remember the words of our Saviour *"Truly I say to you, as you did it to one of the least of My brethren, you did it to Me"* (Matthew 25:40). This being so *"It is more blessed to give than to receive"* (Acts 20:35). Giving to God is gaining from God as *he who sows sparingly will also reap sparingly, and he who sows bountifully will also reap bountifully* (2 Corinthians 9:6).

E. OUR SERVICE AS PRIESTS

When we considered our supplication as priests, we considered our bringing people to God in prayer. Yet this is only one side of the coin as regards the mediatorial service of the priesthood of all believers. A priest not only brought people before God, but he also, as it were, brings God before people. Both aspects of this can be seen in Peter's statement quoted earlier 1. Worship 2. Witness:-

1. *a holy priesthood to offer spiritual sacrifices to God* (1 Peter 2:5)

2. *a royal priesthood ... that you may declare the wonderful deeds of Him Who called you out of darkness into His marvellous light* (1 Peter 2:9).

The greatest service which we can do for anyone is to lead them into the full joy of God's salvation. This should be the burden of our prayers and lives, even if we are not called into "full time Gospel service," and are naturally shy by disposition. Sharing the Gospel brings heaven to earth, the love of God to sinful men. How much do all need to be saved! How much do all need to come to know the Saviour Who alone can meet this need of salvation. Gospel service is priestly service. Paul spoke of *the priestly service of the Gospel of God* (Romans 15:16). Let us then seek His help and strength to fulfil our priestly calling, and, 'in our small corner' and in an unspectacular way, seek to tell others of the love of God in Jesus Christ which we ourselves have experienced. It is both a comforting and a convicting thought that Christ, by His Holy Spirit has consecrated us as priests. *You have been anointed by the Holy One* (1 John 2:20). Have we consecrated our lives back to Him in return?

> *Thy life was given for me*
> *Thy blood O Lord, was shed*
> *That I might ransomed be*
> *And quickened from the dead*
> *Thy life was given for me*
> *What have I given for Thee?*

CHAPTER SEVEN

The Fragrance Of The Sanctified Pieces

(The Tabernacle and its Furniture)

...make of these a sacred anointing oil ... and you shall anoint with it the tent of meeting and the ark of the testimony, and the table with all its utensils, and the lampstand and its utensils, and the altar of incense, and the altar of burnt offering with all its utensils and the laver and its base; you shall consecrate them, that they may be holy
(Exodus 30:25-29).

Here then, we see that the 'tent of meeting,' better known as 'the tabernacle,' along with its furniture, was permeated with a beautiful fragrance - a fragrance owed to its being anointed and thus consecrated with God's special anointing oil.

1. THE SPACE DEVOTED TO THE TABERNACLE

The space devoted to the tabernacle in the five books of Moses would appear at first sight to be out of all proportion. Moses takes just two chapters to describe the creation of the whole universe, in Genesis 1 and 2. Surely this was an awesome event if ever there was one. Yet Moses devotes the whole of Exodus 25-31 and 35-40 to the minute details concerning the tabernacle. As the ultimate author of these chapters is not Moses but God - *All Scripture is inspired by God* (2 Timothy 3:16) - Who used Moses as His mouthpiece, surely we should take heed to the Divine emphasis which, as far as space is concerned, considers the tabernacle over six times more important than Creation.

2. THE SIGNIFICANCE DENOTED BY THE TABERNACLE

The tabernacle was a large tent and the centre of Israel's religious life at this time. It was a portable and provisional sanctuary where, in gracious condescension, God met with His people. God said to Moses *let them make Me a sanctuary, that I may dwell in their midst. According to all that I show you concerning the pattern of the tabernacle, and of all its furniture, so shall you make it* (Exodus 25:8,9).

God had earlier promised to Israel through Moses *I will take you for My people and I will be your God* (Exodus 6:7). As the tabernacle instructions were given, God made another promise *I will dwell among the people of Israel, and will be their God* (Exodus 29:45). He kept His promise! God did actually come down from heaven to dwell in the midst of His people. The details of the tabernacle end with the glorious climax, *Moses finished the work. Then the cloud covered the tent of meeting, and the glory of the Lord filled the tabernacle* (Exodus 40:34).

3. THE SPIRIT'S DIDACTION USING THE TABERNACLE

With New Testament hindsight we can see that the tabernacle was the first link in the chain of the Divine revelation concerning God's dwelling with His people. The revelation was thus *precept upon precept, precept upon precept, line upon line, line upon line, here a little there a little* (Isaiah 28:13). God's Holy Spirit never revealed everything at once, but only as much as the world was ready to receive. Revelation has a progression. The tabernacle eventually was replaced by the temple. But even the magnificent temple was dwarfed in time as *the Word became flesh and dwelt* (lit. 'was tabernacled') *among us, full of grace and truth, we have beheld His glory, glory as of the only Son from the Father* (John 1:14). That was the purpose of the tabernacle. It was part of the preparatory and progressive Divine revelation, preparing us for the present day when God actually dwells personally, by His Holy Spirit in the Christian - *Do you not know that your body is a temple of the Holy Spirit within you..* (1 Corinthians 6:19). And what is true of the Christian individually, is true of the Church corporately. The Church is *a holy temple in the Lord ... a dwelling place of God in the Spirit* (Ephesians 2:22). Could anything be more glorious? Yes! The best is still to come:-

The final link in the chain of truth will not come until the new heaven and the new earth when the joyous cry will be *Behold, the dwelling of God is with men. He will dwell with them and they shall be His people, and God Himself will be with them* (Revelation 21:3). So we see the links. The Sanctuary - the Saviour - the Saint - the Celestial.

THE TABERNACLE'S TESTIMONY TO THE TRUTH

The tabernacle speaks loudly of Christ - the One Who in the fullness of time 'became flesh and pitched His tent among us' (c.f. John 1:14). The tabernacle was anointed with oil, and all of its parts speak of the Anointed One - the Christ of Whom Moses wrote (John 5:46). Let us then step into the fragrant tabernacle and look around. Following the order given in our opening text, what do the separate, sanctified and scented pieces teach us about our Saviour? *Jesus has been counted worthy of much more glory than Moses as the builder of the house has more honour than the house* (Hebrews 3:3).

4. THE SAVIOUR DEPICTED IN THE TABERNACLE

Our text gives us six fragrant pieces of furniture in the following order:- the ark; the table; the lampstand; the altar of incense; the altar of burnt offering and the laver:-

i. The Ark: Christ's Propitiation

Everything in the tabernacle pointed towards the Ark. The Ark, housed in the holy of holies, was the very focal point of Israel's worship, as it was exactly here, that God Himself dwelt in a special way - His omnipresence notwithstanding. God said *There I will meet with you, and from above the mercy seat, from between the two cherubim that are upon the ark of the testimony* (Exodus 25:22).

The Ark was a wooden rectangular box, overlaid with gold. It contained the 10 Commandments, inscribed on two tables of stone. Its cover was also of solid gold and was called the "mercy seat." Springing from the ends of this were two golden cherubim with outstretched wings. Let us apply these details:-

The Law of God, contained in the Ark, is the great demonstration of the holiness of the God Who gave it. The Law of God however is bad news for us, as it demonstrates that we are sinners. The law is God's standard, and we have not reached it. *If it had not been for the law, I should not have known sin* (Romans 7:7). *For whoever keeps the whole law but fails in one point has become guilty of all of it* (James

2:10). We have broken God's law. How could the Israelites, and how can we ever approach this holy God therefore? Only by blood. Sin is so serious that it brings death to the sinner - yet in His mercy God ordained in those Old Testament days a way in which the sinner could approach Him if a substitute died in his place, paying for his sin. Thus the blood of an innocent animal was shed.

Blood, refers to the life being given in death instead of the sinner. Aaron was thus commanded to *take some of the blood ... and sprinkle it with his finger on the front of the mercy seat .... and before the mercy seat he shall sprinkle the blood with his finger seven times* (Leviticus 16:14). The blood thus sprinkled turned aside God's holy wrath - the affront caused by His broken law - and gave the sinner peace with God; the blood gave the sinner atonement.

What a picture of Christ is here! He is our mercy seat! His blood shed on the cross turns aside the wrath of God against us, *making peace by the blood of His cross* (Colossians 1:20). His blood is our propitiation! *Whom God put forward as a propitiation by His blood, to be received by faith* (Romans 3:25). *We are now justified by His blood, much more shall we be saved by Him from the wrath of God* (Romans 5:9).

> *He sprinkled with the blood*
> *The mercy seat above*
> *For justice had withstood*
> *The purposes of love*
> *But justice now withstands no more*
> *And mercy yields its boundless store*

The blood covered mercy seat. It speaks of the propitiation Christ made. The shadow was central to Israel's religion. The substance now fulfilled in Christ is the very heart of the Christian Gospel.

ii. The Table: Christ's Provision

The table in the tabernacle's holy place was known as the 'table of shewbread.' Each Sabbath, twelve loaves were placed on it, one for each of the twelve tribes of Israel. These loaves speak of sustenance - sustenance for Israel in the barren, unyielding wilderness. This is indeed so of Christ to us in the barren wilderness of this world. He said *I am the bread of life. He who comes to Me shall not hunger and he who believes in Me shall never thirst* (John 6:35). Christ alone can provide the necessary bread for eternal life - His Own self. *The bread which I shall give for the life of the world is My flesh* (John 6:51).

Thou art the bread of life
O Lord to me
Thy holy Word the truth
that saveth me

Give me to eat and live
with Thee above
Teach me to love Thy truth
for Thou art love

iii. The Lampstand: Christ's Perfection

The lamp of the tabernacle had seven branches and was hammered out of pure gold, and intricately decorated with flowers and buds. Apart from this the holy place would have been in total darkness, and the priests would thus have had to grope around in the dark. How necessary physical light was - but how much more necessary is the spiritual light of Christ! Jesus said *I am the light of the world. He who follows Me will not walk in darkness but will have the light of life* (John 8:12).

Heaven will be basking in the eternal light of the presence of the God Who is light - but only because on the Cross Christ conquered the darkness of sin and death for all who believe in Him. Jesus is our light, both in this dark world and eternally. Nothing can extinguish this light. *The light shines in the darkness, and the darkness has not overcome it* (John 1:5). Light, in the Bible, symbolises the perfection of God Himself as *God is light and in Him is no darkness at all* (1 John 1:5). Christ's claim to be 'the Light' is thus another pointer to His superlative perfection and Deity.

iv. The Altar of Incense: Christ's Petition

This small golden altar stood in front of the curtain which screened the holy of holies from the holy place. Incense was burnt on it - continually. *Aaron shall burn fragrant incense on it; every morning ... he shall burn it a perpetual incense before the Lord* (Exodus 30:7,8).

We have already considered how incense symbolises prayer ascending to God. Here again we have a reminder of Christ our great High Priest - *He always lives to make intercession for us* (Hebrews 7:25).

Leviticus 16:12 informs us that the fire for this incense was taken from the larger altar. This is remarkable as it shows that intercession has its basis in sacrifice. Christ's intercession for us likewise is always on the basis of His death for us. *... we have an advocate with the Father, Jesus Christ the righteous, and He is the propitiation for our sins* (1 John 2:1,2). We glimpse this also in a post-resurrection appearance of Jesus to His disciples. In John 20:19,20 we read *He said to them "Peace be with you." When He had said this He showed them His hands and His side.* Here we see that the peace He imparts is founded upon His wounds.

Jesus, our great High Priest, is interceding for us at this very moment and will do so until we reach the glory!

He ever lives above
For me to intercede
His all-redeeming love
His precious blood, to plead
His blood atoned for every race
And sprinkles now the throne of grace.

v. The Altar of Burnt Offering: Christ's Pardon

This large, bronze altar was the very first piece of furniture one would encounter upon entering the tabernacle. It shows the priority of sacrifice in the Divine order - 'at Calvary's Cross is where you begin, when you come as a sinner to Jesus.'

The burnt offering is the first sacrifice mentioned in the five sacrifices of Leviticus 1-7. There it is described as a *burnt offering, an offering by fire, a pleasing odour to the Lord* (Leviticus 1:9). Such was Christ in both His life and His death. Heaven itself said of Him *Thou art My beloved Son; with Thee I am well pleased* (Luke 3:22). *Christ ... a fragrant offering and sacrifice to God* (Ephesians 5:2).

Sacrifice was integral to the ritual of Israel. It was also integral to the fuller reality behind all of which the brazen altar spoke since *He has appeared once for all at the end of the age to put away sin by the sacrifice of Himself* (Hebrews 9:26).

vi. The Laver: Christ's Purification

The laver was a large bronze basin of unspecified size. It contained a vast amount of water, and was so constructed that the priests were enabled by it to wash both their hands and their feet. The laver speaks to us of cleansing, and is another type of the truth of Christ. Christ is the cleansing for defiled sinners.

At Calvary *one of the soldiers pierced His side with a spear and at once there came out blood and water* (John 19:34). Here is the promised *fountain opened for the house of David and the inhabitants of Jerusalem to cleanse them from sin and unclean-ness* (Zechariah 13:1). It is Christ Who gives us the *washing of regeneration and renewal* (Titus 3:4) as He *loved the church and gave Himself up for her that He might sanctify her having cleansed her by the washing of water with the word* (Ephesians 5:25,26).

The priests no doubt were prone to defiling themselves in the dusty wilderness. Hence they needed a wash. Sin likewise defiles us in this dusty and dirty world. We too need cleansing, every day. Sin within and without mars our Christian walk, but *If we confess our sins He is faithful and just and will forgive our sins and cleanse us from all unrighteousness* (1 John 1:9).

CONCLUSION

And so we see Christ, the Lord's anointed, in the tabernacle and its anointed furniture. In the fullness of time, the type gave way to the truth, the ritual to the reality and the shadow to the substance. In the tabernacle we see Jesus - our propitiation, provision, illumination, intercession, salvation and purification.

> *Finished all the types and shadows*
> *Of the ceremonial law*
> *Finished what our God has promised*
> *Death and hell no more shall awe*
> *It is finished! It is finished!*
> *Saints from hence your comfort draw.*

CHAPTER EIGHT

The Fragrance Of The Shared Partnership

Behold, how good and pleasant it is when brothers dwell in unity! It is like the precious oil upon the head, running down upon the beard, upon the beard of Aaron, running down the collar of his robes!
(Psalm 133:1,2).

INTRODUCTION

Continuing our study of the Bible's fragrant texts, we see that God's Word declares unity and harmony among brethren to be both *good and pleasant*. That is a pertinent description, as often in life, things that are good for us are not always pleasant, and the things that are pleasant are not always good for us. For example, surgery and visits to the dentist are good for us, even vital - yet they can be painful rather than pleasant. Likewise, ice cream and basking in the sun are both very pleasant - but one is high in calories and the other can cause skin cancer, both of which are not good. Here however, we see that 'fellowship' is both *good and pleasant,* good and pleasant from both the Divine and human perspective.

How sweet, how heavenly is the sight
When those who love the Lord
In one another's peace delight
And so fulfil His Word.

Secondly, our text tells us that peace and harmony amongst brethren *is like the precious oil upon the head, running down upon the beard ... of Aaron, running down on the collar of his robes*. This tells us what actually we already know; that unity and harmony and common friendship and fellowship are one of life's most precious, peerless, priceless and perfumed gifts. How luxuriant and fragrant it is - it is a gift that money just cannot buy.

1. THE CALAMITY OF ALIENATION

The Christian Gospel is God's antidote to the deepest and direst problem that this world knows - the problem of sin. Sin is the root cause of all disunity and disharmony and it has two undesirable effects:- i. Alienation and separation from God ii. Alienation and isolation from each other. We see this very plainly in the sin of our first ancestors, the effects of which we have all too obviously inherited. Eden was a haven of peace and harmony until sin entered the scene. Before the Fall, Adam and Eve enjoyed perfect fellowship with both their Maker and one another. Afterwards however *the man and his wife hid themselves from the presence of the Lord God among the trees of the garden* (Genesis 3:8), fearful of God's holy scrutiny - and with good reason. Then the second effect of sin was/is a mutual disharmony and suspicion as regards one another: Adam blamed his wife for the whole situation, Eve blamed the serpent and then in the very next chapter we see that this ravaging disharmony caused by sin was passed on to Adam's children - *Cain rose up against his brother Abel, and killed him* (Genesis 4:8). So sin has both a vertical and a horizontal effect; it ruins our relationship with God and it ruins are relationships with one another.

2. THE REMEDY OF RECONCILIATION

The Christian Gospel is God's Own antidote and Divine initiative to our alienation both from Himself and each other. In a nutshell, *God was in Christ reconciling the world to Himself, not counting their trespasses against them* (2 Corinthians 5:19). Sin is the seemingly insurmountable barrier between us and God, yet in His amazing grace, God has broken down the barrier of sin by His Son, restoring us to Himself. He did this by sending His Son to actually take our sins upon Him, for we read *He Himself bore our sins in His body on the tree* (1 Peter 2:24). On the Cross, Christ shed His blood for the forgiveness of our sins; this being so, Paul could affirm *But now in Christ Jesus you who once were far off have been brought near in the blood of Christ* (Ephesians 2:13) and could testify *we also rejoice in God through our Lord Jesus Christ through Whom we have now received our reconciliation* (Romans 5:11).

3. THE HARMONY OF PARTICIPATION

A less publicised effect of the Gospel, is that it is God's antidote and remedy for our alienation and isolation from each other. Salvation, of course, is an individual act, as no one can be saved 'by proxy,' - we have to trust Christ as our own, personal Saviour. But salvation does not end there. When God saves us He unites us to *the body of Christ* (1 Corinthians 12:27 et al) and brings us into *the household of God* (1 Timothy 3:15) - the Church. The Church is the community of the redeemed.

True New Testament Christianity is corporate and communal as well as individual. It knows no such thing as an isolated Christian. The Church is one body, united by a common living faith in Christ; and this unity transcends this life into the next.

> *Blest be the tie that binds*
> *Our hearts in Christian love*
> *The fellowship of kindred minds*
> *Is like to that above*

4. THE SERENITY OF RESTORATION

If the Bible has one theme, it is that of God's restoration of the Paradise of Eden - Paradise Lost, Paradise Regained. This culminated in Christ and will be consummated in Christ, of Whom it is written *in Him all the fullness of God was pleased to dwell, and through Him to reconcile to Himself all things, whether on earth or in heaven, making peace by the blood of His cross* (Colossians 1:19,20). It is Christ Who is and will be the source of all unity and harmony, as it is God's *purpose which He set forth in Christ as a plan for the fullness of time, to unite all things in Him, things in heaven and things on earth* (Ephesians 1:10).

i. The Divine Friendship

With the coming of Christ, we see reconciliation in action. Initially He chose twelve disciples, included amongst whom were Matthew the tax-collector - in league with the hated Romans, and Simon the Zealot - a Jewish militant extremist, keen to shake off the Roman yoke. Because of Jesus, these two enjoyed table fellowship. Such an occurrence, humanly speaking, should not have happened.

Today, we live in a divided world. These words are actually being written from the sectarian riven city of Belfast, Northern Ireland. Yet the first century was also divided. The main division was between Jew and Gentile - yet in Christ this division was broken down. We see this in Acts 10. Peter was a good Jew. Cornelius was a Roman Centurion. The two were poles apart socially, but God saw otherwise. Peter testified *"You yourselves know how unlawful it is for a Jew to associate with or to visit any one of another nation; but God has shown me that I should not call any man common or unclean"* (Acts 10:28).

Next, see the diverse makeup of the church at Antioch. *Barnabas, Simeon who was called Niger, Lucius of Cyrene, Manaen a member of the court of Herod the tetrarch and Saul* (Acts 13:1). What a mixture of black, white, educated and uneducated, strict Pharisee and pagan Gentile! It gives the ring of truth to Paul's words to the churches in the nearby Province of Galatia:- *There is neither Jew nor Greek, there is neither slave nor free, there is neither male nor female; for you are all one in Christ Jesus* (Galatians 3:28). How potent the Gospel therefore is! Humanly speaking, the gulf between Jew and Gentile was unbridgeable, but *what is impossible with men is possible with God* (Luke 18:27). It is possible because of Christ. *For He is our peace, Who has made us both one, and has broken down the dividing wall of hostility.... that He might create in Himself one new man in place of the two, so making peace, and might reconcile us both to God in one body through the cross, thereby bringing the hostility to an end* (Ephesians 3:14,15,16).

ii. The Divine Family

A metaphor used for God's reconciled community is that of *members of the household of God* (Ephesians 2:19, 1

Timothy 3:15). This tells us much. It illustrates the glorious truth of Christian adoption, i.e. that God takes those who are by nature hell-bound children of wrath, and transforms them into heaven-bound children of God. Through Christ, God actually adopts us into His family, bestowing on us all the rights and privileges of being the King's children. *See what love the Father has given us, that we should be called children of God; and so we are* (1 John 3:1).

Adoption is both individual and corporate. Christians have Christ as their elder Brother. Staggeringly *He is not ashamed to call them brethren* (Hebrews 2:11). Christians can know and call God by the intimate *Abba, Father* (Romans 8:15); the family prayer is noteworthy in that it opens on the corporate note *Our Father Who art in heaven* (Matthew 6:9). Christians can also call each other "brother" and "sister." These are the New Testament family terms for those in God's family. We call ourselves this because we are so! Of course, the best of families have their quarrels and differences, but nothing can undo the blood tie. Likewise, Christ said of His church:- *the powers of death shall not prevail against it* (Matthew 16:18). The Church has an indestructible blood tie. It is *the church of God which He obtained with the blood of His Own Son* (Acts 20:28).

iii. The Divine Fellowship

A particularly rich word used to describe the *good and pleasant* unity which we are considering it that of "fellowship." Fellowship is variously translated as "to have in common," "sharing," "participation" and "communion." We read that the first century believers *devoted themselves to the apostles' teaching and fellowship, the breaking of bread and the prayers* (Acts 2:42). This fellowship is visibly expressed when believers from all walks, positions, stations, ages and stages of life gather around the Lord's Table for "Communion" in obedience to the Lord's command. There, on the table is one loaf, symbolic of the Lord's body. There also on the table is one cup, symbolic of *My blood of the new covenant which is poured out for many for the forgiveness of sins* (Matthew 26:28). And so Paul wrote to the very diverse Corinthian church, composed of Jew and Greek, slave and free:- *The cup of blessing which we bless, is it not a participation in the blood of Christ? The bread which we break, is it not a participation in the body of Christ? Because there is one bread, we who are many are one body, for we all partake of the one bread* (1 Corinthians 10:16,17).

Unfortunately, the word "fellowship" can be devalued, and degenerate into refering to the general "chuminess" of the secular world. Genuine Christian fellowship however is always a fellowship in and with God, through Christ by the Holy Spirit. There can be no 'horizontal' fellowship if the 'vertical' is missing. Thus John wrote *so you may have fellowship with us; and our fellowship is with the Father and with His Son Jesus Christ* (1 John 1:5). It is a fellowship in the light, as *God is light* (1 John 1:5), *and if we walk in the light as He is in the light we have fellowship with one another* (1 John 1:7).

Christian fellowship is a great and glorious blessing. The present writer has been blessed with it in all four nations of the United Kingdom as well as overseas. In Jerusalem today, one can even see Jew and Arab on their knees, praying together to the One God through Christ. Such a happening staggers and confounds the authorities.

iv. The Divine Fullness

At this point, an objector may point out the all too obvious disharmony of the Church. This is a fact that cannot be ignored. Churches are divided into denominations, and even impeccably orthodox, Bible-believing churches can suffer division amongst its own ranks:- 'To live above with saints we love will certainly be glory; to dwell below with saints we know well, that's another story!'

The root of the matter is still sin. The church is a community of the redeemed, and the redeemed are forgiven sinners - yet sinners nevertheless. Sin will never be completely rooted out in this life, thus total harmony is reserved for the church triumphant in heaven - a truly multi-national and multi-denominational gathering, *from every nation, from all tribes and peoples and tongues* (Revelation 7:9).

The church's best life is yet to be! Notice John's glimpse of her in the new heaven and the new earth *prepared as a bride adorned for her husband* (Revelation 21:2). Significantly he also sees that *the sea was no more* (Revelation 21:1). The sea separates. It is a divider of nations. Sin of course separates too, and even the happiest of churches can be infiltrated and divided by false teaching, suspicion, hostility and personality clashes. What a prospect then that in heaven the sea of sin and division will be no more! The church then will be one harmonious and symphonious band, united in her praise to the God Who saved her and the God Who loves her. Until then, let us:-

1. rejoice in the reconciliation God has made in Christ and

2. do all we can towards the harmony of God's family, *forbearing one another in love, eager to maintain the unity of the Spirit in the bond of peace* (Ephesians 4:2,3) and

3. anticipate the glorious prospect of the completion of our redemption, when we will dwell together in the sinless state in the land of endless day, in perfect harmony and peace with God and one another forevermore. We will then experience:-

v. The Divine Fragrance

How good and pleasant it is when brothers dwell in unity! It is like the precious oil upon the head, running down upon the beard, upon the head of Aaron, running down on the collar of his robes (Psalm 133:1,2).

> *How good a thing it is*
> *How pleasant to behold*
> *When brothers learn to live at one*
> *The law of love uphold*
>
> *As perfume by its scent*
> *Breathes fragrance all around*
> *So life itself will sweeter be*
> *When unity is found.*

CHAPTER NINE

The Fragrance Of The Sister's Preparation

The anointing of Jesus by Mary at Bethany was a literally fragrant incident - as well as being very tender and touching. John records that when it happened *the house was filled with the fragrance of the ointment* (John 12:3). Jesus said of Mary's action *"truly, I say to you, wherever the Gospel is preached in the whole world, what she has done will be told in memory of her* (Mark 14:9). His prophecy was fulfilled. The Holy Spirit has ensured that this lovely incident has been recorded for us no less than three times in the Bible, in Matthew 26:6-13; Mark 14:3-9 and John 12:1-8.

Let us then consider this *woman (who) came up to Him with an alabaster flask of very expensive ointment* (Matthew 26:7). Mary's action and sweet smelling sacrifice speaks far louder than words. The Bible says *faith by itself, if it has no works, is dead* (James 2:17). Mary's action here is telling evidence of her loving devotion to Christ. Hers was no dead faith. She sacrificed her wealth and even her reputation in service to her Master. Mary's action teaches us much, and the spirit of it is surely an example for us to emulate. But let us consider from the fragrance of this sister's preparation:-

1. **HER PERCEPTION OF THE CHRIST OF GOD :
   DESCRIPTION**
2. **HER PICTURE OF THE CROSS OF GOLGOTHA:
   DEPICTION**
3. **HER PATTERN OF THE CHRISTIAN'S GOAL :
   DEVOTION**

1. HER PERCEPTION OF THE CHRIST OF GOD

Mary ... anointed the feet of Jesus (John 12:3).

"Anointing was an ancient custom ... The practice was in use, not only as part of the ceremony in connection with the coronation of kings (see 2 Kings 11:12) and at the installation of the High Priest (Psalm 133:2), but as an act of courtesy and hospitality toward a guest." (MANNERS AND CUSTOMS OF THE BIBLE, James M. Freeman; Bridge Publishing Company; 1972; p.219). Mary knew the worthiness of the One Who had raised her brother Lazarus to life. Accordingly, she anointed Him.

i. Burial

Jesus commended Mary's action - and such a commendation is higher than all the awards that this passing world can ever offer. He said *she has done a beautiful thing to Me ... she has done it to prepare Me for burial* (Matthew 26:10,12). For *burial!*

Mary's perception of both the Person and Work of Christ here was so right - which is more than can be said for certain men! When Jesus first mentioned the Cross to Peter, Peter responded *God forbid, Lord! This shall never happen to You!* To which Jesus replied *Get behind Me, Satan! You are a hindrance to Me; for you are not on the side of God, but of men* (Matthew 16:22,23). Similarly, on the road to Emmaus, the risen Christ gave the rebuke *O foolish men, and slow of heart to believe all that the prophets have spoken! Was it not necessary that the Christ should suffer these things* ... (Luke 24:25,26). Mary, however, had it absolutely right. Her action was anticipatory of Christ's death. How did she get such insight then? Scripture does not tell us directly, but we know from Luke 10:39 that this same *Mary sat at the Lord' sfeet and listened to His teaching.* What a testimony! *Truly one thing is needful. Mary has chosen the good portion* (Luke 10:42) - and surely sitting at Jesus's feet and listening is our needful thing and good portion too. Thus the Saviour Himself taught Mary, and she had an ear to hear.

We today are to be taught by the Scriptures, and the Spirit of God illuminating the Scriptures to us. This will give us the Mary-like perception of Christ. The Spirit of God uses the Scriptures of God to bear witness to the Son of God to the saved of God leading to the song of God - *Worthy is the Lamb Who was slain!* (Revelation 5:12).

Mary knew that Christ was born to die - which was more than Peter knew at that stage. *The wages of sin is death* (Romans 6:23), *Christ died for our sins* (1 Corinthians 15:3). This being so *she ... anointed My body beforehand for burying* (Mark 14:8).

ii. Balming

She has anointed My body ... (Mark 14:8), said Jesus. Mary's action here betrayed that she knew her Lord as her "Anointed One" - her Messiah, her Christ! Mary, of course, did not have the benefit of the New Testament Scriptures then as we do now. Yet the Old Testament anticipated and prophecied One Who would come as the Agent of God to redeem His people. The Christ would be a prophet, priest and king, and Jesus the Christ surely is all three in His One blessed Person:-

1. *I will raise up for them a prophet ...* (Deuteronomy 18:18)
2. *You are a priest forever ...* (Psalm 110:4)
3. *I have set my king on Zion, my holy hill ... You are My Son, today I have begotten You ...* (Psalm 2:6,7).

Jesus, my Shepherd, Husband, Friend
My Prophet, Priest and King
My Lord, my Life, my Way, my End
Accept the praise I bring

2. HER PICTURE OF THE CROSS OF GOLGOTHA

The treasures of Scripture are not always on the surface. Sometimes they have to be dug and mined. Consider the heart of this fragrant incident at Bethany. *Mary took a pound of costly ointment of pure nard and anointed the feet of Jesus and wiped His feet with her hair; and the house was filled with the fragrance of the ointment* (John 12:3). Mark adjusts his angle slightly, and records that Mary *came with an alabaster flask of ointment of pure nard, very costly, and she broke the flask and poured it over His head* (Mark 14:3). Can you see the picture of the Cross of Golgotha here? Consider the stages:- the precious, purest nard was taken; the flask was broken; the ointment was poured and the pleasantest of effects ensued as *the house was filled with the fragrance of the ointment*. A blessed container was broken and it became a blessing! That is an exact picture of the Cross of Golgotha! The flask was broken and the precious ointment was outpoured. At Golgotha, the precious body of the Lord Jesus was broken and His blood outpoured - and what an eternal fragrance ensued! We must look at this in greater detail. Notice that the nard was pure, precious, poured and perfumed:-

A. PURE NARD

...a pound of costly ointment of pure nard, (John 12:3) was the substance taken. The Lord Jesus was infinitely and immaculately pure. We cannot find a stain in Him. His virgin birth, virtuous life, vicarious death and victorious resurrection are all one in the volume of the Book. He is the sinless Christ. *He committed no sin* (1 Peter 2:22), *This Man has done nothing wrong* (Luke 23:41).

B. PRECIOUS NARD

... ointment of pure nard, very costly (Mark 13:3). There are a few "precious things" in the Bible. Peter said that *faith is more precious than gold* (1 Peter 2:4). Even more precious though is the Christ of our faith. He is *that living stone, rejected by men but in God's sight chosen and precious* (1 Peter 2:4). Peter continues *to you therefore who believe, He is precious* (1 Peter 2:7).

Surely the most precious substance in all the world, to the Christian, is the blood of Christ. It is this blood which attained our redemption. It is more than precious, as the cost of our redemption was priceless. Peter says concerning this precious, priceless substance:- *You know that you were ransomed from the futile ways inherited from your fathers, not with perishable things such as silver or gold, but with the precious blood of Christ,like that of a lamb without blemish or spot* (1 Peter 1:18,19). This, and this alone is our *like precious faith* (2 Peter 1:1, KJV).

C. POURED NARD

she broke the flask and poured it over His head (Mark 14:3). It was precisely the same with the Lord Jesus. The communion service reminds us of this so vividly:- *this is My body which is broken for you* (1 Corinthians 11:24). *This is My blood of the new covenant which is poured out for many for the forgiveness of sins* (Matthew 26:28).

Glory be to Jesus
Who in bitter pains
Poured for me the life blood
From His sacred veins

Grace and life eternal
in that blood I find
Blest be His compassion
Infinitely kind

D. PERFUMED NARD

The house was filled with the fragrance of the ointment (John 12:3). There was no blessing without the breaking, and no perfume without the pouring. Similarly, the Bible says *without the shedding of blood there is no forgiveness of sins* (Hebrews 9:22). Yet on the cross, Christ's precious blood was shed, bringing the perfume of redemption to all who believe, for *in Him we have redemption through His blood, the forgiveness of our trespasses according to the riches of His grace* (Ephesians 1:7).

On the Cross Christ *offered Himself without blemish to God* (Hebrews 9:14) and this offering was fragrant and infinitely pleasing to Him. Christ loved us *and gave Himself up for us a fragrant offering and sacrifice to God* (Ephesians 5:2). It was a wonderful fragrance to God - and it is a wonderful fragrance to us, as it brings our eternal salvation. However, what is a wonderful fragrance to the believer is a woeful fragrance to those who reject Christ. Paul gives the warning *we are the aroma of Christ to God among those who are being saved and among those who are perishing, to one a fragrance from death to death, to the other a fragrance from life to life* (2 Corinthians 2:15,16).

3. HER PATTERN OF THE CHRISTIAN'S GOAL

The whole of this lovely incident exudes Mary's devotion. Mary gives us a description of the true Christ/Anointed One; she gives us a description of the Cross which was impending, but she also gives us an example of devotion to emulate. Her devotion to Christ knew no bounds. She considered it nothing to spend 300 denarii on her Lord at one go. A denarius was a day's wage for a labourer, thus in one moment she spent the greater part of a years' wages on her Lord. We are reminded of king David's words in her devotion to great David's Greater Son *I will not offer burnt offerings to the Lord my God which cost me nothing* (2 Samuel 24:24). Jesus gave His all for us, the minimum we can give in return is our all to Him. Notice though:-

i. The Sinner's Scornful Condemnation

Judas Iscariot... said, "Why was this ointment not sold for 300 denarii and given to the poor?" This he said, not that he cared for the poor but because he was a thief, and as he had the money he used to take what was put in it (John 12:5,6). Judas thus sought to rob God. He sought to stop the honour and devotion being given to Jesus. Shamefully, it is the same today. Unbelievers and even believers can rob Jesus of the honour, time, energy, service, love, devotion and praise which is both His due and delight.

Mark records that *there were some who said to themselves indignantly "Why was the ointment thus wasted?"* (Mark 14:4). This is a typical reaction of unbelief towards the worship of Jesus. No sacrifice is too great for Jesus. The worship of Him is even more vital than good and noble deeds to our fellow men - not that there is a conflict between the two. Nothing is ever wasted when it is devoted to Christ. *He who sows bountifully will reap bountifully* (2 Corinthians 9:6).

ii. The Saviour's Sweet Commendation

She has done a beautiful thing to Me ... Truly, I say to you, wherever the gospel is preached in the whole world, what she has done will be told in memory of her (Mark 14:6,9).

Mary of Bethany comes over in a wonderful light in Scripture. Whenever we read of her, she is at the feet of Jesus! In Luke 10:39 she *sat at the Lord's feet and listened to His teaching.* In John 11:32, at the death of her brother Lazarus, *Mary, when she came where Jesus was and saw Him, fell at His feet.* And in the incident here, *she anointed the feet of Jesus and wiped His feet with her hair* (John 12:3). Mary was always at the feet of Jesus! - at His feet waiting, weeping or worshipping! So should we be too. Her devotion is for us to emulate. Mary honoured Jesus - the Jesus Who alone is worthy of all honour - and Jesus honoured Mary and gave her a place in the Book of God and the God of all books, the Holy Bible. It is engraved forever in Scripture for us to read as *The grass withers, and the flower falls, but the Word of the Lord abides forever* (1 Peter 1:24,25). Truly, no devotion to Christ is ever a waste. May we too, like Mary and Paul, *count everything as loss because of the surpassing worth of knowing Christ Jesus my Lord* (Philippians 3:8).

> *We sing the praise of Him Who died*
> *Of Him Who died upon the Cross*
> *The sinner's hope, let men deride*
> *For this we count the world but loss*

CHAPTER TEN

The Fragrance Of The Saviour's Passion

*And walk in love, as Christ loved us and gave Himself up
for us, a fragrant offering and sacrifice to God*
(Ephesians 5:2).

THE APOSTLES'S LETTER

Paul's letter to the Ephesians has been termed 'the quintessence of Paulism,' and its six chapters really do distil for us the wonders of the full-orbed Christian Gospel. This letter, (notwithstanding the fact that scholars are unsure as to whether it was written as a circular to the churches of Asia Minor, including Ephesus, or to the Ephesians exclusively) reveals much of *the unsearchable riches of Christ* (3:8) available to poor sinners, along with the glorious truth that it is *By grace you have been saved through faith, and this is not your own doing, it is the gift of God - not because of works, lest any man should boast* (2:8,9). Fittingly, grace has been defined as God's Riches At Christ's Expense.

Ephesians has a beautiful symmetry to its six chapters. Chapters 1-3 unfold and extol the wonderful grace of God in Christ to us - *He has blessed us in Christ with every spiritual blessing in the heavenly places* ...(1:3); whilst chapters 4-6 encourage us to live out the practical implications of this grace of God in Christ and so *lead a life worthy of the calling to which you have been called...* (4:1). The verse we are considering has a similar symmetry. Paul says that doctrine determines duty/belief determines behaviour, in that the personal experience of Christ's love for us should result in our reciprocal love to God and others by way of response:- *walk in love as Christ loved us...* (Similarly, at the end of chapter 4 he says that we should be forgiving people, as in Christ we are a forgiven people.)

THE AMAZING LOVE

Every believer has an infinite debt to the sacrificial, saving love of Christ - the very love mentioned here in Ephesians 5:2. In 3:19 Paul tells us *the love of Christ surpasses knowledge* - and indeed it will take an eternity just to begin to plumb its depths. Yet our verse gives us a glimpse of three aspects to Christ's amazing love for us. These are:-

1. CHRIST'S LOVE CAME FIRST : IT WAS PRIOR
2. CHRIST'S LOVE CAME FORGIVING : IT WAS PARDONING
3. CHRIST'S LOVE CAME FRAGRANT : IT WAS PERFUMED

1. CHRIST'S LOVE CAME FIRST : IT WAS PRIOR

Walk in love as Christ loved us ... The hymnwriter in experiencing this 'first love' of Christ was enabled to pen the words "I've found a Friend, oh such a Friend, He loved me ere I knew Him ..." articulating the thoughts of all true believers. John, the beloved disciple, was in total agreement with Paul's emphasis when he wrote *we love because He first loved us* (1 John 4:19) and *In this is love, not that we loved God but that He loved us and sent His Son to be the propitiation for our sins* (1 John 4:10).

Christ's love came first. He died for us on the cross before any of us were ever even born - yet we were in His mind and on His heart as He hung and suffered there. Jesus once said *Greater love has no man than this, that a man lay down his life for his friends* (John 14:13). Jesus did more. He layed down His life for His enemies. *God shows His love for us in that while we were yet sinners Christ died for us ... while we were enemies we were reconciled to God by the death of His Son*..(Romans 5:8-10). Christ's perfect love for us preceded our imperfect love for Him. Christ's love came first; it was prior, but notice secondly:-

2. CHRIST'S LOVE CAME FORGIVING : IT WAS PARDONING

Christ loved us and gave Himself up for us ... Where would we ever be apart from the giving and forgiving love of Christ? It is a theme which runs right through the New Testament as well as filling heaven itself with a paean of praise. In 5:25 of this letter Paul states *Christ loved the church and gave Himself up for her...* Paul opens his letter to the Galatians proclaiming *our Lord Jesus Christ Who gave Himself for our sins to deliver us from the present evil age..* (Galatians 1:3). Then Paul reminded Titus of the Christ *Who gave Himself for us, to redeem us from all iniquity ...* (Titus 2:14).

This giving and forgiving love of Christ was both for the church corporately and the believer individually. The best of all is to be able to echo Paul's words in Galatians 2:20 from the heart and say Christ *loved me and gave Himself for me*. A Christian is far from perfect, but praise God that a Christian is fully pardoned; pardoned through the blood of Christ *Who loves us and has freed us from our sins by His blood* (Revelation 1:5).

> *Was it the nails Oh Saviour,*
> *that bound Thee to the tree?*
> *No ' twas Thine everlasting love,*
> *Thy love for me, for me.*

Christ's love, it came first, it came forgiving and pertinently for our study:-

3. CHRIST'S LOVE CAME FRAGRANT : IT WAS PERFUMED

Christ loved us and gave Himself up for us a fragrant offering and sacrifice to God.

Christ's sacrificial love is and will be infinitely delectable to the Christian, as it is the cause of the believer's eternal salvation; but perhaps less well known is the fact that Christ's sacrifice at Calvary was also infinitely pleasing to God the Father:- *Christ ... through the eternal Spirit offered Himself without blemish to God ...* (Hebrews 9:14), or, as our verse puts it, His sacrifice was a fragrant offering to God.

The term 'fragrant offering,' or 'sweet smelling savour' (KJV) simply means that Christ's sacrificial death was well-pleasing to God the Father, totally acceptable to Him, satisfying His holy law in full. The first time this term is used in Scripture is in Genesis, back in the time of Noah, when *Noah offered burnt offerings and the Lord smelled the pleasing odour...* (Genesis 9:21). Then if we turn to Leviticus 1-7, we see there that three of the five offerings there (namely the burnt, cereal and peace offerings) are described as *sweet savour offerings,*- and all three cast light on the Ultimate Sacrifice offered by Christ at Calvary:-

1. In the burnt offering we see Christ's perfect consecration - a fragrant offering
2. In the cereal offering we see Christ's perfect character - a fragrant offering
3. In the peace offering we see Christ's perfect communion - a fragrant offering.

Interestingly though, the remaining two offerings, i.e. the sin and trespass offerings, are not described as 'sweet savour offerings.' This shows that God is not pleased with sin and that it demands punishment by death; hence at Calvary, the skies were darkened, and God hid His face from His Son when *For our sake He made Him to be sin Who knew no sin so that in Him we might become the righteousness of God* (2 Corinthians 5:21).

CONCLUSION

Christ's death was a fragrant offering, the sweetest savour of the sweetest Saviour. We remind ourselves again of that touching episode in John 12, when Mary, expressing her devotion to her Lord took and broke that pound of costly ointment of pure nard and anointed Jesus's feet. *The house was filled with the fragrance of the ointment* (John 12:3). The pure, precious, peerless Son of God was broken on the cross of Calvary, and His precious life-blood was poured out as a fragrant offering to God. It was indeed fragrant to God, so fragrant and pleasing that He raised His Son from the grave three days later. It is also exceedingly fragrant to us, as it is *the aroma of Christ ... a fragrance from life to life..* (2

Corinthians 2:16). Let us then seek to *Walk in love, as Christ loved us and gave Himself up for us, a fragrant offering and sacrifice to God.*

O the wonders of His love
See Him coming from above
To atone and die for thee
Praise Him, praise Him cheerfully

Yes, with joy we'll praise Him now
Till with saints above we bow
And to all eternity
Praise Him, praise Him cheerfully

APPENDIX

THE FRAGRANCE OF THE SCENTED PRODUCE

We began our study with a consideration of the special, sacred and scented produce described and detailed in Exodus 30 - the holy anointing oil. *The Lord said to Moses, "Take the finest of spices : of liquid myrrh five hundred shekels, and of sweet smelling cinnamon half as much, that is two hundred and fifty, and of aromatic cane two hundred and fifty, and of cassia five hundred according to the shekel of the sanctuary, and of olive oil, a hin; and you shall make of these a sacred anointing oil blended as by the perfumer, a holy anointing oil it shall be* (Exodus 30:22-25). It is with this sacred anointing oil that we shall now draw our fragrant studies of our most fragrant Saviour to a close.

Oil, in the Bible, is often used as a symbol for the Holy Spirit. 1 Samuel 16:13, for instance, reads *Samuel took the horn of oil, and anointed him (David) in the midst of his brothers, and the Spirit of the Lord came mightily upon David from that day onward.* It is most important to note however that the Holy Spirit does not draw attention to Himself; rather,

He always points away and directs our focus to Christ. Jesus said of Him *He will glorify Me, for He will take what is Mine and declare it to you* (John 14:14). The Holy Spirit's role thus is primarily to bear witness to Christ, *that in everything He might be pre-eminent* (Colossians 1:18). Paraphrasing the Shorter Catechism, it is the Holy Spirit Who makes us partakers of the redemption purchased by Christ by His effectual application of Christ's Work to and in our souls. "The Spirit applieth to us the redemption purchased by Christ by working faith in us, and thereby uniting us to Christ in our effectual calling." (cf. Questions 29 and 30).

It comes as no surprise that when we analyse the anointing oil's ingredients, we see glimpses of our Saviour - He of Whom it is written *Therefore Your God has anointed you with the oil of gladness above Your fellows; Your robes are all fragrant with myrrh and aloes and cassia* (Psalm 45:7,8). Let us now analyse the five ingredients of the oil, these *finest of spices* and see what their scent tells us of *Him Whom the Father consecrated and sent into the world* (John 10:36).

1. LIQUID MYRRH

His lips are like lilies, distilling liquid myrrh (Song of Solomon 5:13). When the Lord Jesus was yet an infant, some wise men from the East were led to seek Him; and when they had found him, we read *they fell down and worshipped Him. Then, opening their treasures they offered Him gifts, gold and frankincense and myrrh* (Matthew 2:11). What fitting presents for the Son of God these were! Gold tells us of His Deity; frankincense speaks of His priestly office; and myrrh, even at this early stage, tells us that Jesus was born to die, as myrrh was used to embalm dead bodies. *Christ Jesus came into the world to save sinners* (1 Timothy 1:15) says a precious text, and He did so by dying in the place of sinners on Calvary's cross. Myrrh featured early in Jesus's life; and myrrh featured at its seeming close, as after He died, *Nicodemus ... came bringing a mixture of myrrh and aloes about a hundred pounds' weight. They took the body of Jesus, and bound it in linen cloths with the spices, as is the burial custom of the Jews* (John 19:39,40).

2. SWEET SMELLING CINNAMON

Cinnamon is an aromatic spice derived from the bark of a cinnamon tree. It is used to give flavour to food and wine (c.f. *spiced wine to drink* ,Song of Solomon 8:2). In Biblical times cinnamon was highly prized, and it is included on the list of expensive commodities valued by fallen Babylon in Revelation 18:13.

It is Jesus Who gives the 'spice' to our lives. Ordinary and plain though they may be, it is the love of Jesus that makes all the difference. He said *I came that they may have life, and have it abundantly* (John 10:10) and *These things I have spoken to you that My joy may be in you, and that your joy may be full* (John 15:11). Everything about our Saviour exudes an exquisite fragrance - His character, His compassion, His conduct and His cross. He is *distinguished among ten thousand ... His cheeks are like beds of spices, yielding fragrance ... His speech is most sweet, and He is altogether desirable* (Song of Solomon 5:10,13,16).

3. AROMATIC CANE

The exact nature of this aromatic wood has been lost in antiquity. Scholars cannot shed much light upon it apart from speculation. We know however that wood was used in early sacrifice, even before Moses. Isaac, that great type of Christ asked *Behold, the fire and the wood; but where is the lamb for a burnt offering?* (Genesis 22:7). The Lamb was eventually to die on a cruel, callous wooden cross. *He Himself bore our sins in His body on the tree* (1 Peter 2:24). This indeed was aromatic cane; it was *a fragrant offering and sacrifice to God* (Ephesians 5:2). The Divine delight in this offering (c.f. the *Lord smelled the pleasing odour* Genesis 8:21) was underscored by Christ's resurrection from the dead:- *They put Him to death by hanging Him on a tree; but God raised Him on the third day and made Him manifest* (Acts 10:39,40).

4. CASSIA

Again, the scholars are uncertain as to the exact origin of this spice. Etymologically, the Bible often mentions accacia wood, but whether there is a connection cannot be proved. The evidence suggests that cassia was derived from a certain bark, and this was used in later times at funerals - so again we are reminded of the death of our Saviour. Our ultimate blessing is derived from the Work of the Cross, not the wood of the Cross. The importance is not the emblem but the expiation. *Christ redeemed us from the curse of the law having become a curse for us, for it is written, "Cursed by every one who hangs on a tree"* (Galatians 3:13). Again, Psalm 45:8 states of Christ *Your robes are all fragrant with myrrh, aloes and cassia.* The fragrant formula reminds us of the lovely fragrance of Jesus in all its parts. The final important ingredient was:-

5. OLIVE OIL

Olive oil was a staple in Biblical times. It was used for food, light (i.e. burned as fuel in lamps) and medicine. Jesus too is our spiritual food and light, as well as the great physician of our souls. If olive oil was essential for life, how much more essential is Jesus for eternal life! Interestingly, the blessing of this oil was gained by the bruising/crushing of the olive. Extracting the oil was a long, slow process. A tree would be beaten so its olives would fall off. These olives would then be put into a large stone press and a mill stone would then be put on top of them. This stone would then be harnessed to an animal who walked in circles blindfolded. In the process the olives would be crushed and the oil would ooze out and be tapped. Thus there was no blessing apart from this bruising.

All of the above was literally true of our Saviour too. Our blessing derives from His bruising. He went from the olive press of Gethsemane to the old rugged cross of Golgotha, and there *He was wounded for our transgressions, He was bruised for our iniquities ... and with His stripes we are healed* (Isaiah 53:5). As some fragrant plants do not yield their sweet perfume unless they are crushed, likewise, if our Saviour had not been so crushed at Calvary, He could not have yielded His sweetest pardon.

Jesus Christ is alive today! He is now enthroned at the Father's right hand in heaven; the crucified One is the crowned One - yet even today He still sends His Holy Spirit on sinful, lost men and women, and gives them His special anointing - an anointing which opens blind eyes (c.f. John 9:6 ff) and applies the work of Calvary to human souls, bringing into the realms of human experience all the blessings of sins forgiven and peace with God for time and eternity. May this self same Holy Spirit help us to love Him and value Him more than we do. May the Lord fill our hearts and homes with THE LOVELY FRAGRANCE OF JESUS!

> *How sweet the name of Jesus*
> *In which we gather now*
> *It lifts the clouds of sadness*
> *From off the careworn brow*

Herein for all the needy
A fullness is revealed
And fragrance round it sheddeth
Like odours sweet unsealed.

Soli Deo Gloria

EPILOGUE

My Beloved speaks and says to me:
"Arise, my love, my fair one,
and come away;
for lo, the winter is past,
the rain is over and gone.
The flowers appear on the earth,
and the time of singing has come,
and the voice of the turtle-dove
is heard in our land.
The fig tree puts forth its figs,
and the vines are in blossom;
they give forth fragrance.
Arise, my love, my fair one,
and come away.
O my dove, in the clefts of the rock,
in the covert of the cliff,
let me see your face,
let me hear your voice,
for your face is sweet,
and your face is comely."

(Song of Solomon 2:10-14).

MY FATHER'S HOUSE
~ *Glimpses of the Glory* ~

Another heartwarming book by Timothy J.E. Cross

"Timothy Cross has written a book in which he gives us 'glimpses of glory' - not merely to satisfy our mental curiosity, but as all good theology is meant to do, to warm our hearts and make us long for it ourselves .... The author has managed to give us a foretaste of the delight that is in store for God's children."

(Rev. Derek Thomas, Minister and Author)

"The author brings to this ... a freshness of writing which is very appealing ... A refreshing and challenging book for all who have been travelling along the pathway of faith or for those who long to begin such a journey to the heavenly home."

Our Inheritance (Protestants Today)

".. very delightful and a joy to all..
".. enjoyed every moment of this, especially the continual backing up of Old and New Testament Scriptures and the sound simplicity and readability.."

(West Wales)

"..I have been blessed by reading the contents..."

(Northern Ireland)

"He writes clearly of such truths without apologising or hiding behind the supposed ignorance of the modern man ... In the simple lessons drawn much of value is to be found about the Saviour's love and God's providential and personal care"

(Believer's Magazine)

"The book does not indulge in any fanciful speculation but is very much Biblically-based and centred.. is relevant to our present position in Christ as well as being an encouragement for the future..
"'My Father's House' is a concise and warmly written book. It is helpful and encouraging to Christians and would also be worth passing on to those who might presently be seeking the Lord Jesus .."

(Church Newsletter)

"Timothy Cross' writing talent is a heaven-sent gift ...."

(South Wales Echo, 8/7/93)